The Scottish Accordion

Will Marshall

To access the online audio go to:
WWW.MELBAY.COM/30858MEB

I0808782

Foreword

Scottish accordion music takes many different forms from folk style, dance music, solo playing and group/ensemble work. Will Marshall captures the essence of how to learn the basics of the instrument with this compendium of tutorial methods designed to educate in a fun, practical way.

The text is informative and is supported with diagrams and graphics that help in the learning process. Helpful fingering techniques for both right and left hands and tips on how to use and control the bellows are essential for creating a fluent playing style, which Will encapsulates perfectly in this book.

Will touches on general theory practices throughout and explains how rhythms are created to accomplish the desired effect for dance music playing. He also includes a selection of his own compositions, which demonstrate styles within the Scottish idiom. The accordion world has been crying out for a concise accordion tutor on Scottish music and this book certainly fits the bill! It will inspire and encourage people from every age demographic to appreciate the versatility of this instrument.

Well done Will on producing an effective learning tool for those interested in playing the accordion...*Scottish Style!*

Ian Muir
Senior Accordion Tutor – Royal Conservatoire of Scotland

Table of Contents

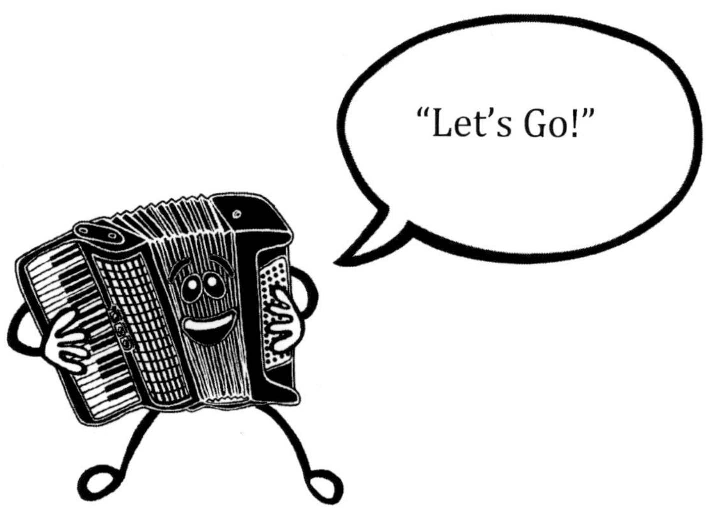

Preface

With this book I wanted to give everyone an insight into playing traditional Scottish music on the accordion. I go into detail about the three main Scottish rhythms, and how to apply them to your own playing.

The online recordings will help you with the exercises. There is an added bonus in the 'Let's Play' chapter where you will be the lead musician and play with a band.

I thank Grant McFarlane, Keith Dickson and Ade Mckenna for their help and input in producing this book.

A special mention must go to Murray Begg for his great Illustrations.

Have fun with this book and enjoy playing the accordion!

Will Marshall

Crotchet = Quarter Note
Quaver = Eighth Note
Semiquaver = Sixteenth Note
Minim = Half Note

The Piano Accordion in Scottish Music

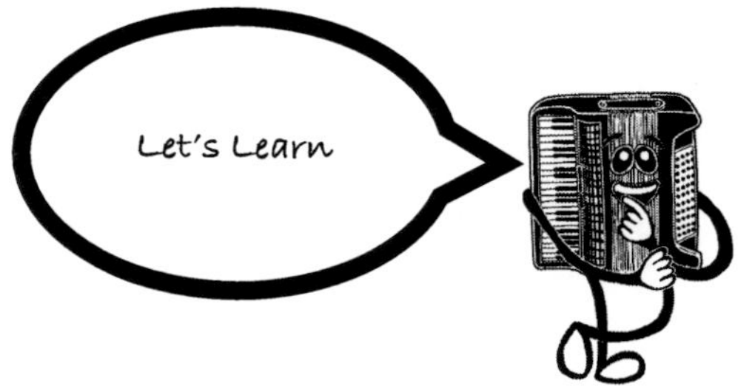

Early Years

By the early 1900s the piano accordion was becoming popular in Scottish music and with Scottish musicians. Prior to the rise in popularity of the piano accordion, the small button accordion was extremely popular throughout Scotland. It was inexpensive, durable and relatively easy to learn to play without any formal training.

Using a piano keyboard instead of buttons on the melody side gave a smoother sound and more advanced harmony. The expanded left-hand side offered more chords and bass notes for accompaniment.

The piano accordion quickly became popular within traditional and modern dance bands at music halls, variety theatres and concert parties. As the principal instrument of a Scottish dance band and accompaniment to popular Scottish song, the piano accordion attracted a lot of musicians.

Scottish Country Dance Band

As with other world cultures, Scotland has a tradition of social dancing with its own music. Such dancing is still a central element of weddings, ceilidhs (pronounced *kay-lees*), gala balls and other social events. The dance band consists of lead accordion, rhythm accordion, fiddle, piano, bass and drums. With the revival of Scottish country dancing between the 1920s and 30s, dance bands were in high demand on radio and TV nationally and around the world. One big star was Sir Jimmy Shand (1908 - 2000) who became widely known for his dance-friendly tempos.

Ceilidh Band

The ceilidh band can have a similar lineup to the Scottish dance band but often includes the addition of guitar, clarsach and bagpipes. A ceilidh band can be much more experimental with the basic, reel, jig and strathspeys to create modern ideas.

If playing at a ceilidh, the band would be more relaxed about playing for dancers and perhaps a little faster than a Scottish dance band.

Popular Ceilidh Dances

Playing for ceilidh dancing is great fun and an exciting way to play with other musicians.

To get you started, here is a list of popular ceilidh dances and what to play for them.

The Dashing White Sergeant (Reels)

Strip the Willow (Jigs)

The Virginia Reel (Reels)

Flying Scotsman (Reels)

Eightsome Reel (Reels)

Gay Gordons (Marches)

Canadian Barn Dance (2/4 or 6/8 Marches)

Military Two Step (6/8 Marches)

St. Bernard's Waltz (3/4 Waltzes)

Folk Music

The accordion is popular within the folk music genre and has the flexibility to be used either as a lead instrument or as a supporting instrument playing chords and harmony.

Artists such as Capercaillie, and Phil Cunningham did wonders for the accordion back in the 80s and 90s. More recently, popular folk-rock bands such as Skippinish and Mànran include the accordion as a featured main instrument.

Listen to all these different genres and notice how the accordion is used in different ways.

The Left Hand

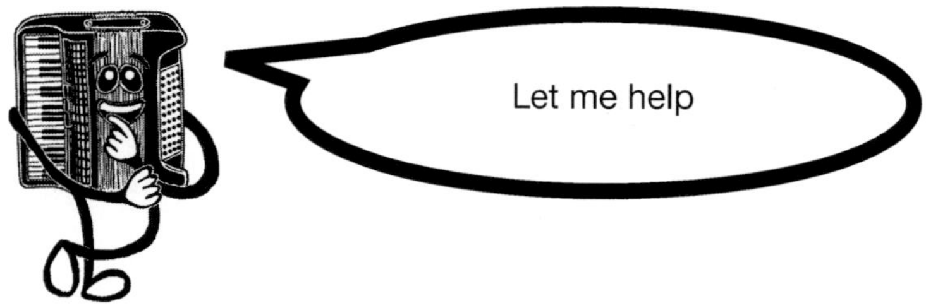

How to Read and Play the Left Hand

Throughout this book, notation is provided for the left hand to help with placement of bass notes and chords. Before you dive into the different chapters on rhythms, it is worth reading this chapter on how to read and play the left hand.

When playing major chords in 2/4, 4/4 and 6/8, use your 4th finger on the bass note and 3rd finger on the chord. If you have one bar of the same chord, alternate the bass note with the button above. The fingering for this would be (4,3,2,3) bass note, chord, bass note, chord.

In the example below, notice how the chord is written an octave higher than the bass note, and written as one note. The chord symbol above tells you what the chord is: Major, minor, 7th or diminished.

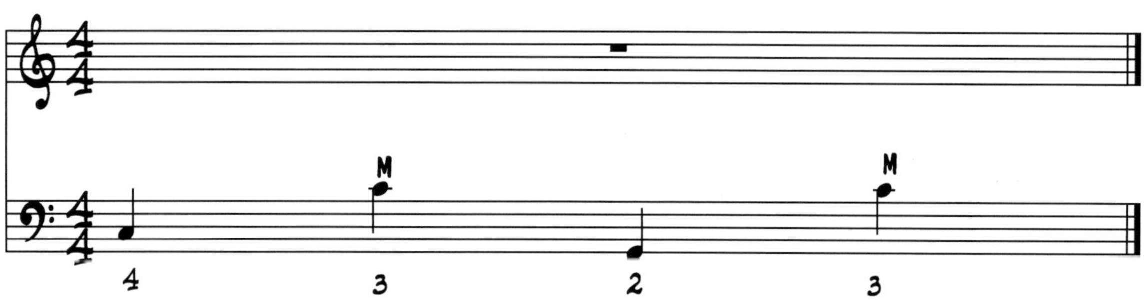

Here is what the notation actually means: You are alternating the bass note, but playing the same chord. This forms a little triangle in the bass.

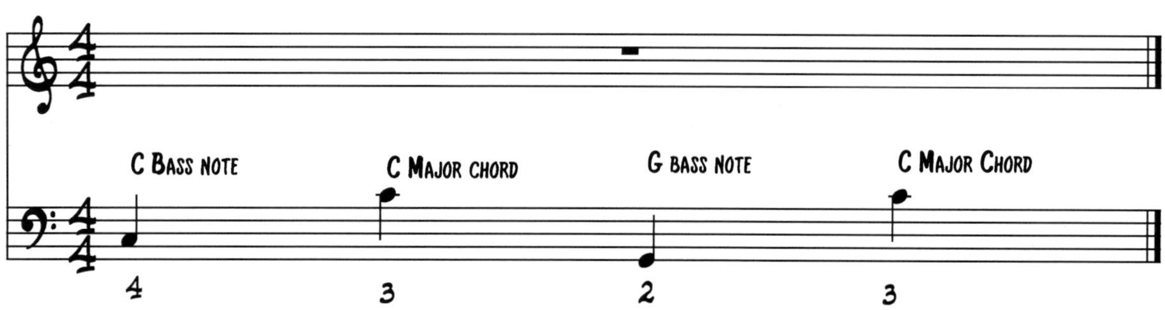

Major Chord

Below is a diagram of a small section of the bass on a full size accordion. If you have a smaller one, you might only have one bass row and not as many chords.

The diagram below is shown as if you are facing the accordion.

Focus on the little triangle you are making with the bass pattern. (4,3,2,3)

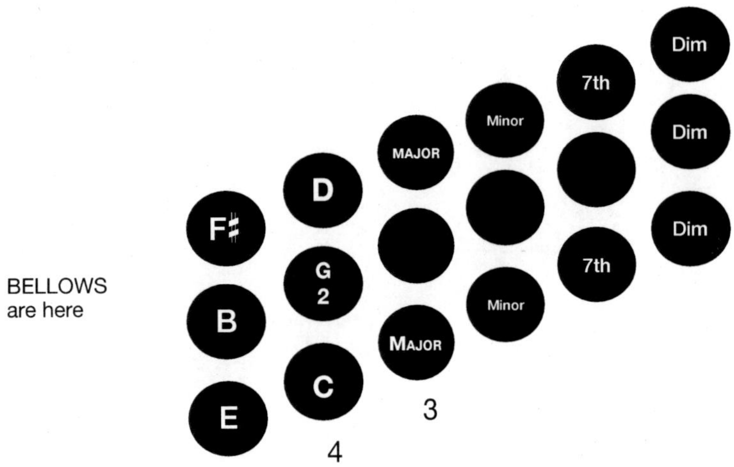

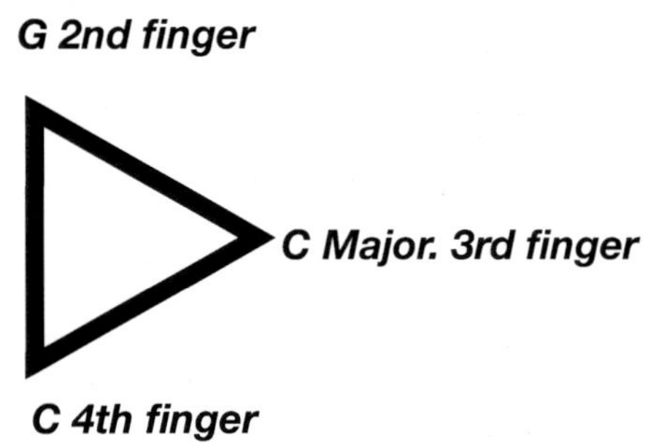

The Left-Hand Triangle

Practice making the triangle and get comfortable playing the bass and chords with a nice, short rhythmic bounce. Move around the bass keyboard and try different bass notes and chords.

Below is a typical example of how the bass you have just played would be notated in a traditional music book. If you see the chord like this, it is implied you play (4,3,2,3)

This book will help you understand how to play the left hand in the different rhythms.

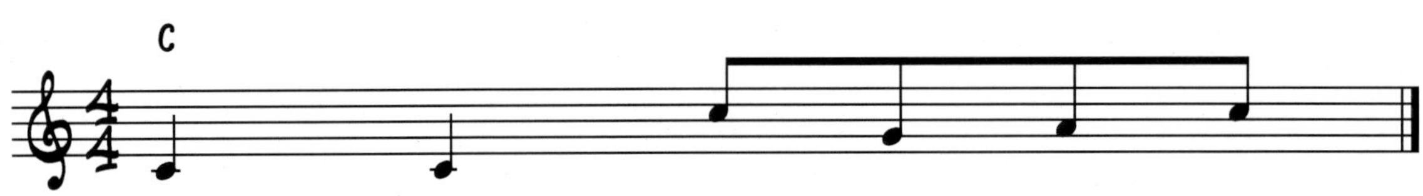

Minor and 7ths

For minor and 7th chords, use your 2nd finger to create a triangle with a different shape.

You can still alternate the bass note, this time with your 3rd finger. Let's look at the next example.

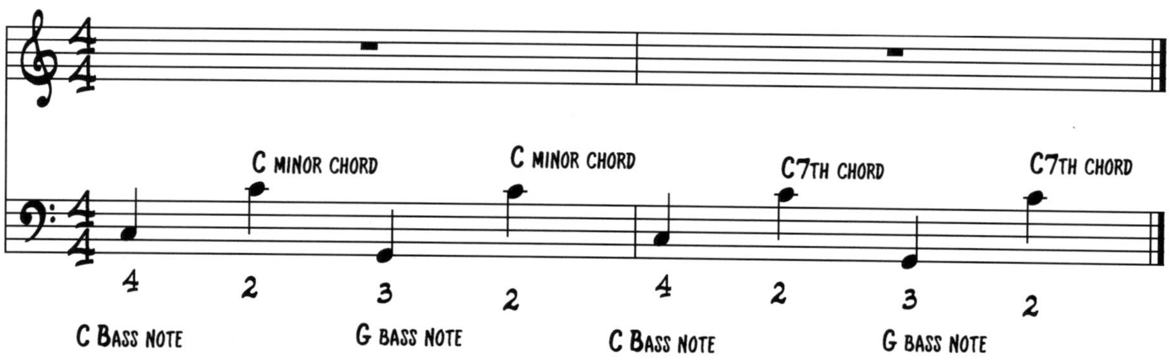

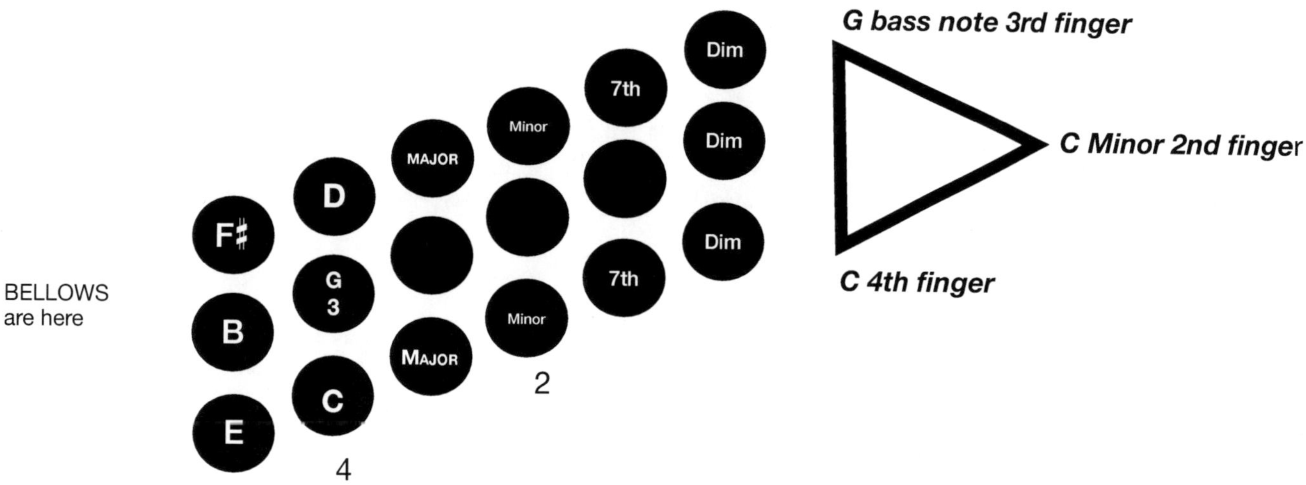

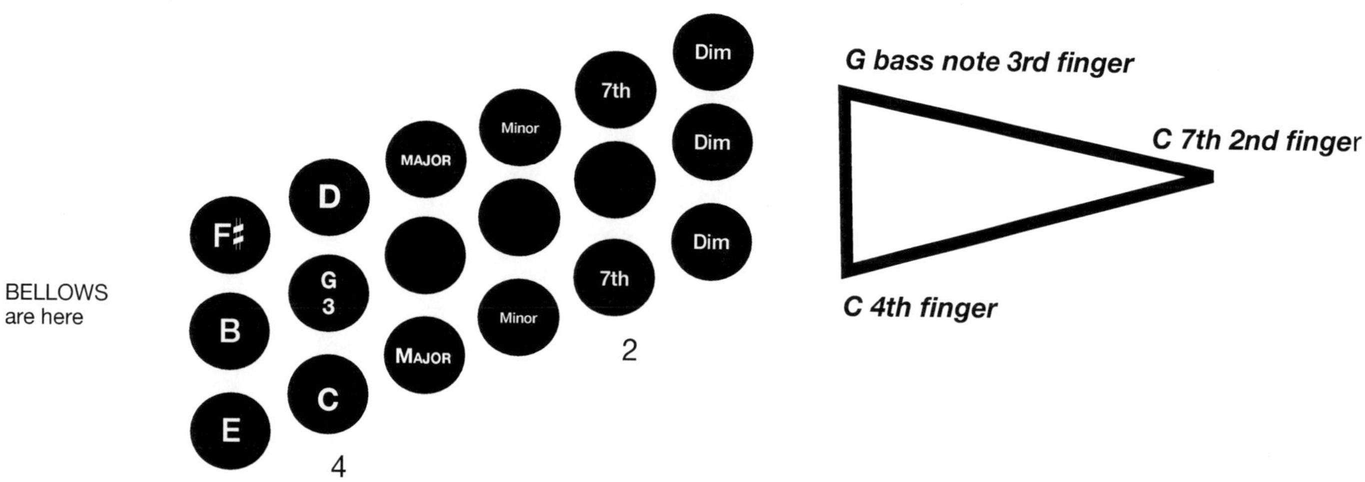

Diminished Chords

Diminished chords are played by making a straight line. Use your 3rd finger on the bass note and 2nd finger on the chord button.

Diminished chords are often used as passing chords within traditional music. For example, G, G♯dim and Amin when the melody allows for this to happen.

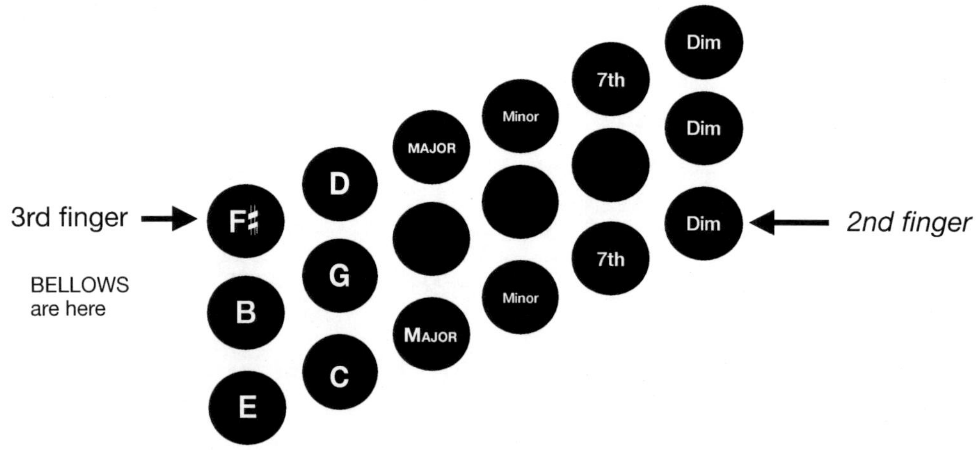

Slash Chords

It is very common to see slash chords within traditional music. They occur when you have a single chord for the whole bar and the composer or arranger has indicated they would like a different bass note than the tonic. Let's look at the example below.

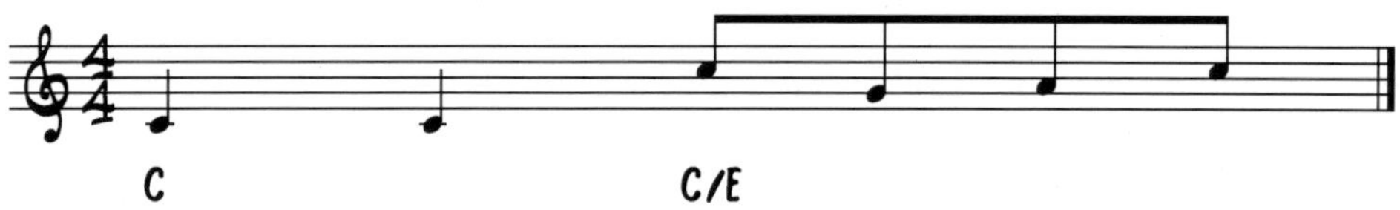

This is how it is played. The C is played as normal. The slash chord tells you that you play an E bass note then a C major chord.

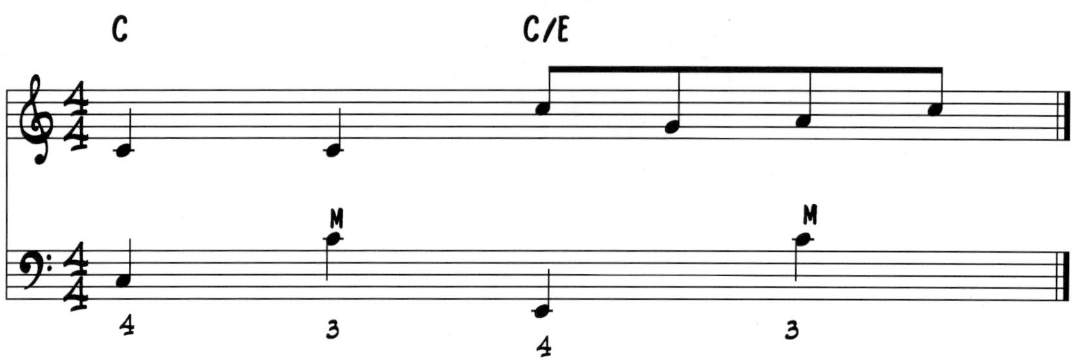

Jig 6/8

"Haggis and Sausages"

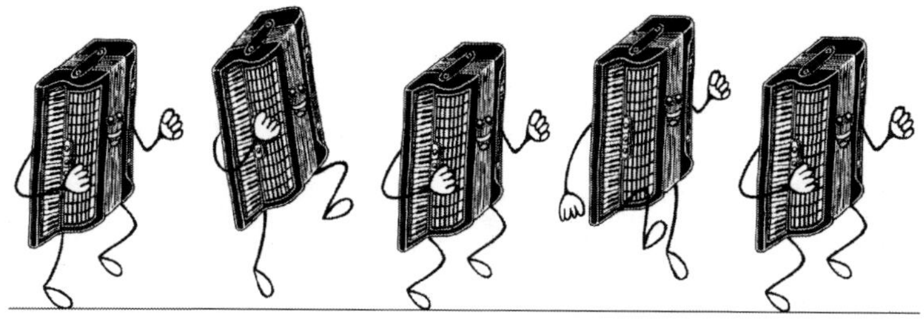

A jig has a skipping feel - let's go!

What is a Jig?

It is a lively tune written in 6/8 time.

The 6 tells us there are 6 beats in the bar, and the 8 tells us it is a quaver beat. So we have 6 quaver beats in the bar.

If you say the phrase "Haggis and Sausages" a few times this will give you an idea of the jig rhythm.

Also, think of a skipping action. Go on, try both!

Let's look at a jig written out in standard accordion notation as you might find it in a ceilidh or traditional music book. The chords may be written above or below the melody line: in the following tune they are above the melody line.

Jig for John

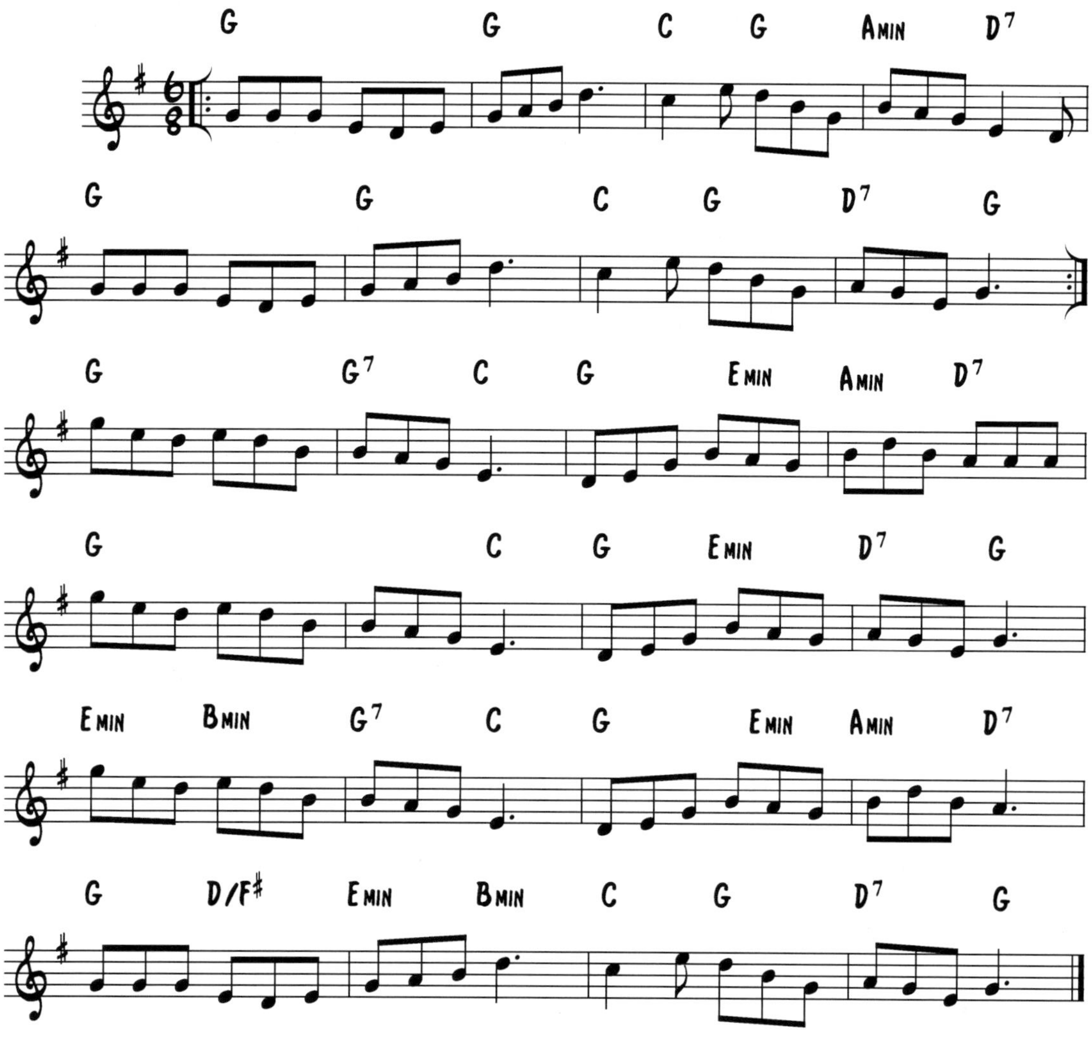

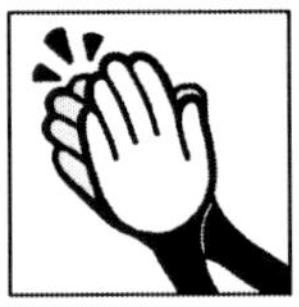

Ex. 1

Track 1

The first thing we need to do is learn how to play the bass in 6/8 time.

Let's try a clapping exercise.

Clap and count to 6. Easy. Now this time count to 6 again, but only clap on 1,3,4 and 6. This is the basic 6/8 pattern for the bass. Look at the music below and then try it on your accordion.

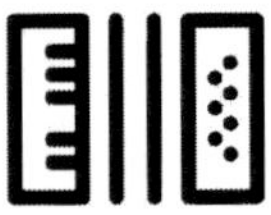

Ex. 2

Track 2

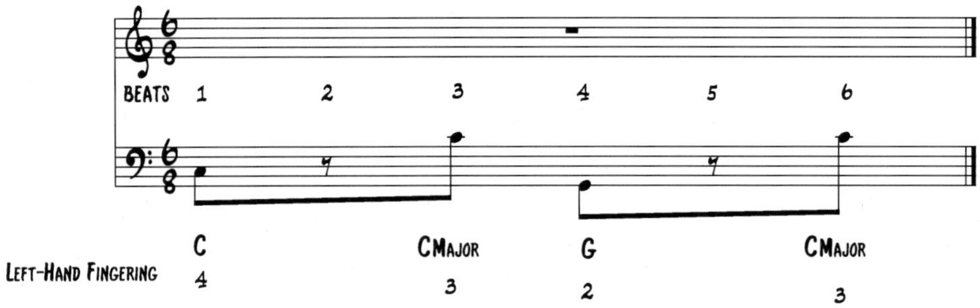

Let's explore this concept further with the bass diagram below.

Use your 4th finger (ring finger) on the C bass note, middle finger (3) on the C major chord, 2nd finger on the G bass note and back again to the 3rd finger for the C major chord. This fingering allows you to alternate the bass notes easily and avoids repetition of the same bass note.

Follow the triangle below using the fingers suggested. Count the beats nice and loud, place the bass on beats 1 and 4 and the chord on beats 3 and 6. Beats 2 and 5 are silent.

Practice this pattern in C major, then you can move on.

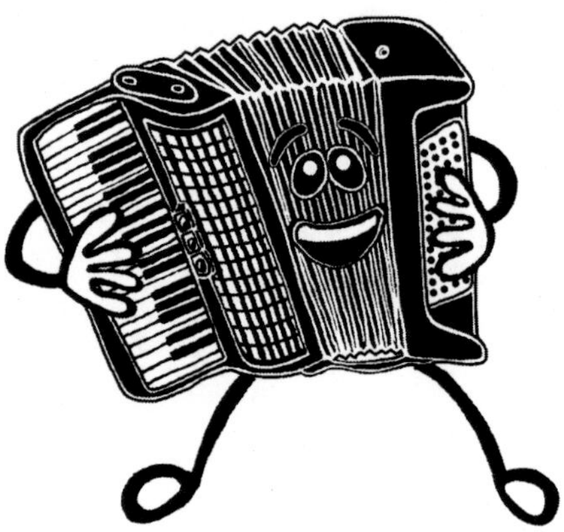

Let me hear you count "1-2-3-4-5-6!"

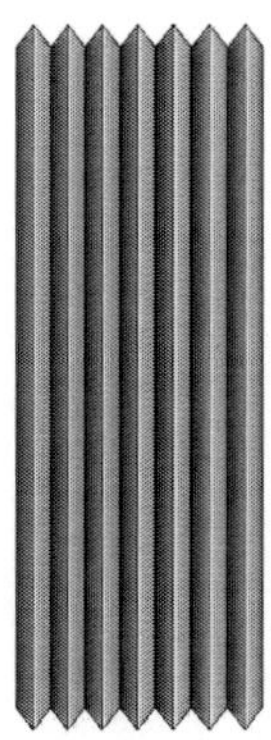

Bellows

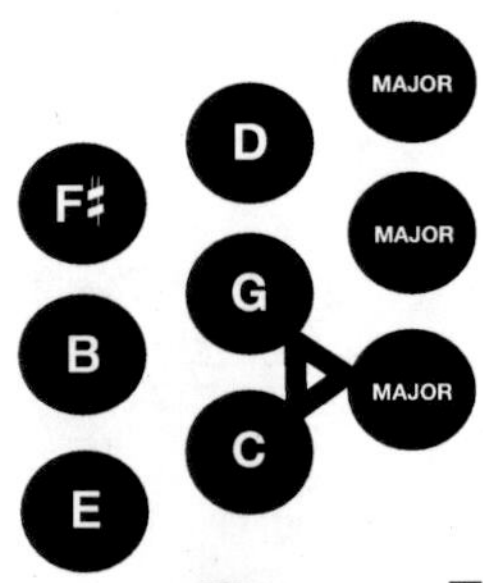

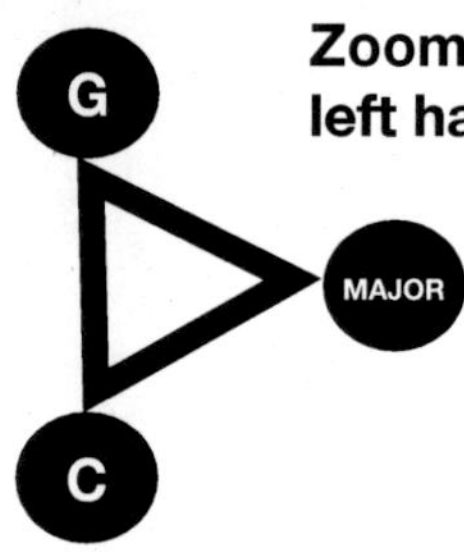

Zoomed in diagram - left hand triangle

Metronome Practice

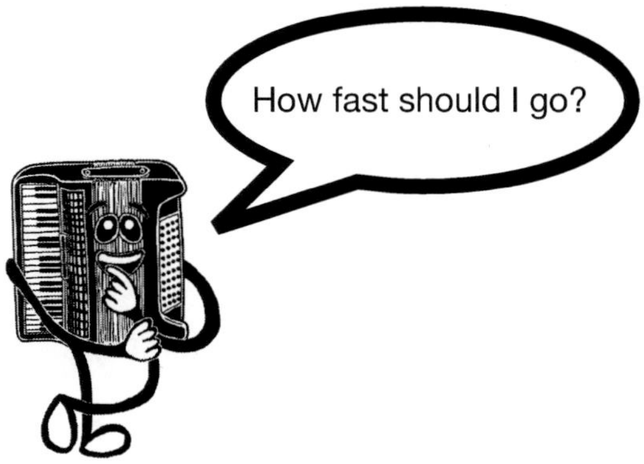

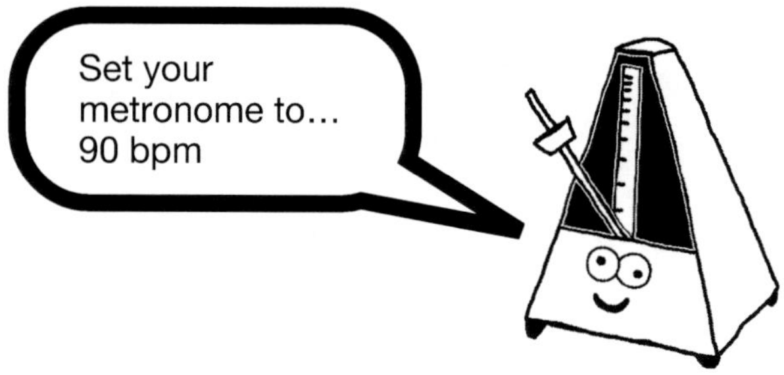

Jigs can vary in speed from 100 to 130 bpm (beats per minute).

When practicing this bass exercise, it is a good idea to set your digital metronome to 6/8 and quaver = 90 bpm. That way you can play the bass on clicks 1, 3, 4 and 6.

This a great exercise as you won't rush playing the bass note or chord. Gradually increase the speed as you master the 6/8 meter.

When you feel comfortable and you are not fighting against the metronome, change the metronome to 2/4. This will give you the '2-in-the-bar feel' without all the individual clicks. The bass note lands on the click and the chord will sound in the gap.

Start at 85 bpm. Gradually increase the speed so you are comfortable with placing the bass notes on the clicks and the chords in the gap.

As beats 1 and 4 are where the bass note lands, they are regarded as the strong beats. On the metronome this is every click in 2/4.

This highlights the '2-in-the-bar feel' you need for jigs. You will learn more about this within the right-hand section.

For your own practice on jigs in this chapter, use the metronome to help you with the rhythm.

As always – GO SLOW!

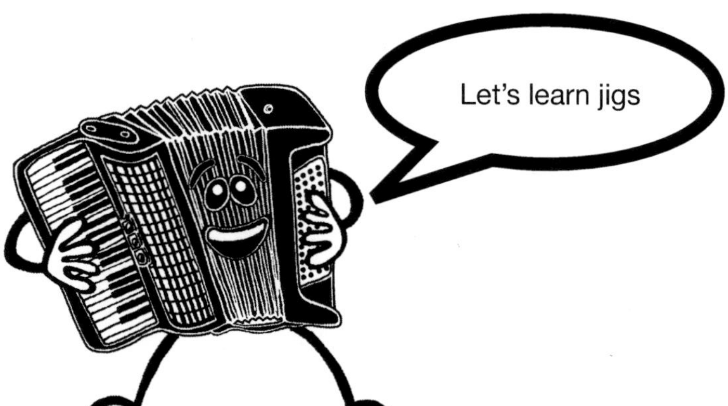

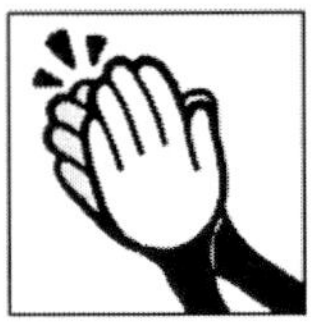

Ex. 3
Track 3

Simple Right-Hand Rhythm

Let's have some clapping fun. Clap the 6 quavers in each bar and say the words in time with every clap.

This will give a better understanding of the next exercise, when you put a right hand melody to the tune. Get comfortable with the rhythm before moving on.

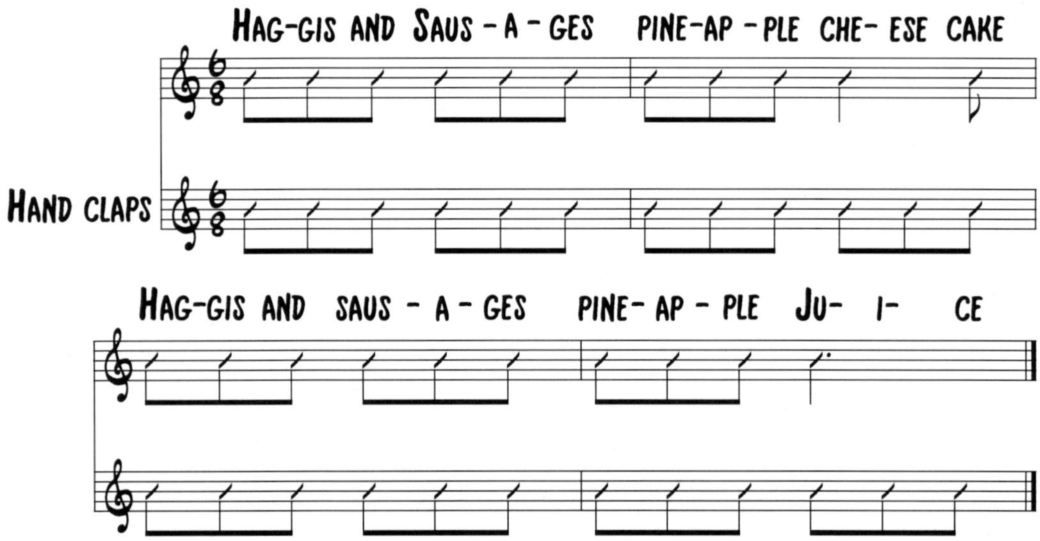

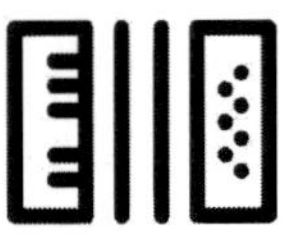

Ex. 4
Track 4

Let's learn your first jig. Using the rhythm you have learned above, you now have a melody to learn.

The fingering is marked to help you focus on keeping the notes nice and smooth – legato.

Count in quavers and use the lyrics to help you.

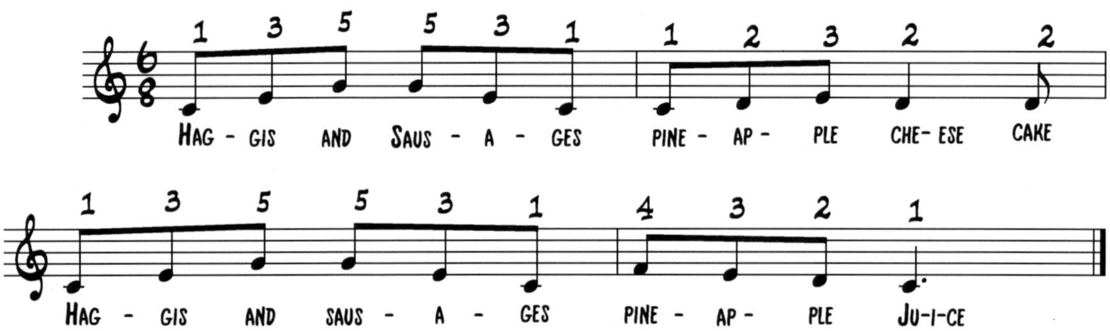

How to Play with Both Hands at Once

Ex. 5
Track 5

With the tune you have now learned, you are going to use both hands together.

Just like the bass exercise in Ex. 2, beats 2 and 5 are silent in the bass.

For this exercise we are going to go very slow.

With both hands, play the first note: Focus on keeping the bass short and the right hand long.

Practice Ex. 5 until you are confident with putting both hands together. Gradually build up the speed before you move on and try the full tune.

Practice Tip!

Think of both hands on a trampoline.

Both hands go down at the same time: however, the left hand springs straight back up and the right stays down much longer.

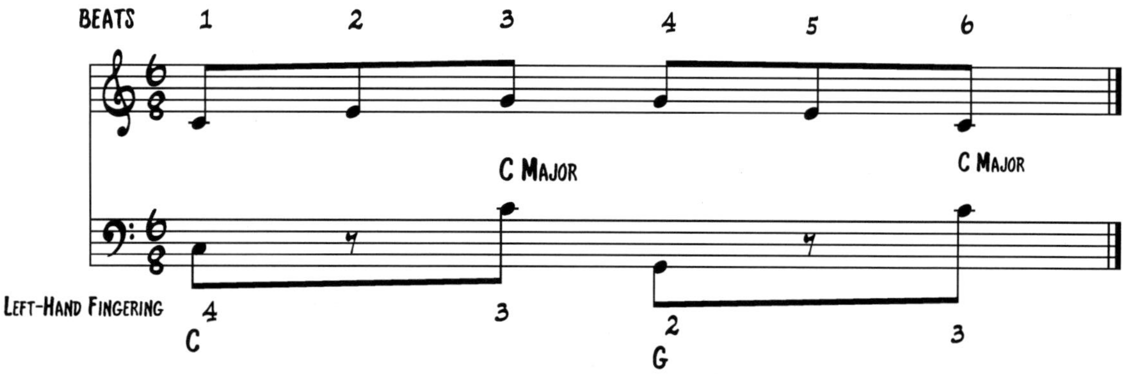

Here is the left-hand part for your jig. Learn this bit first before adding both hands together.

Ex. 6a
Track 6

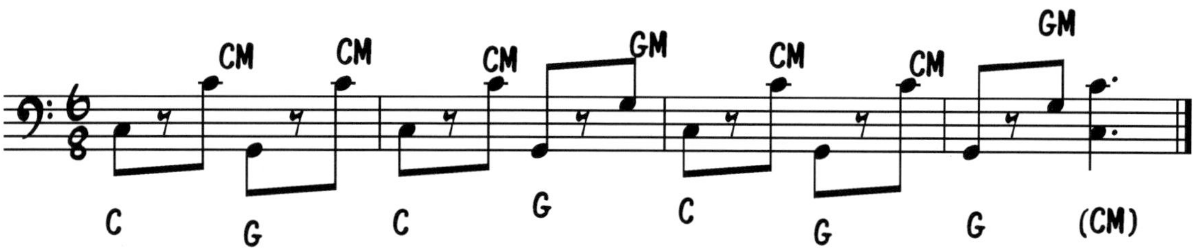

Here are the full 4 bars. Things to look for:

Bar 2: The bass moves up to G major. Also, in bar 2 the crotchet can be tricky to play with the quaver which follows it.

Count the beats from 1 to 6 and make sure you do not move on to the quaver until you have counted beats 4 and 5.

In the last bar, your left hand plays both the bass note and the chord together for 3 counts.

Ex. 6b
Track 7

The crotchet can be tricky. Count!

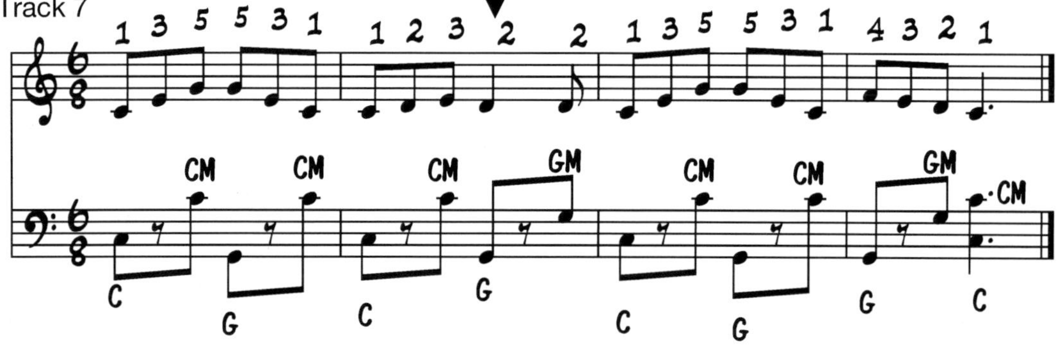

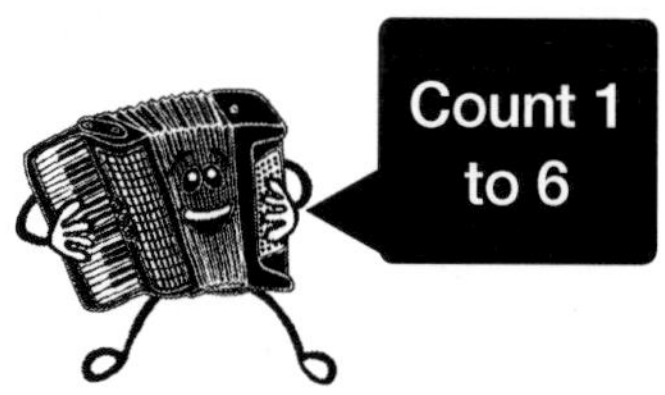

Right-Hand Techniques

Scottish music has a lot of repetition of melody and rhythm.

Let's explore and get your haggis and sausages ready!

The next exercise uses lots of C's. When repeating the same note we can use fingers 1, 2 and back to 1. Practice this slowly and try to make this nice and smooth.

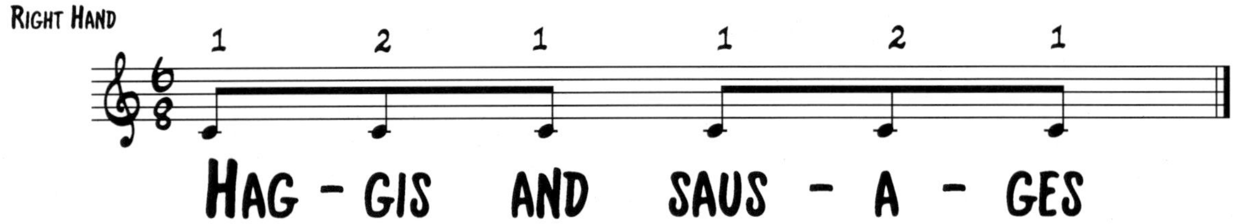

Ex. 7
Track 8

Practice Tip!

When repeating the same note, keep your 1st and 2nd fingers as relaxed as possible and cushioned against the keyboard. Make the notes smooth.

Continue to practice this exercise until you can repeat the notes smoothly. Below is a C major scale. It is helpful to practice your sales with the same 1-2-1-1-2-1 technique.

Practice going slowly up and down the scale a few times with the fingering 1-2-1 twice on each note. Once you are confident in C major, try different keys and scales. Also, try mixing up the sequences: 2-1-2 and 3-1-3.

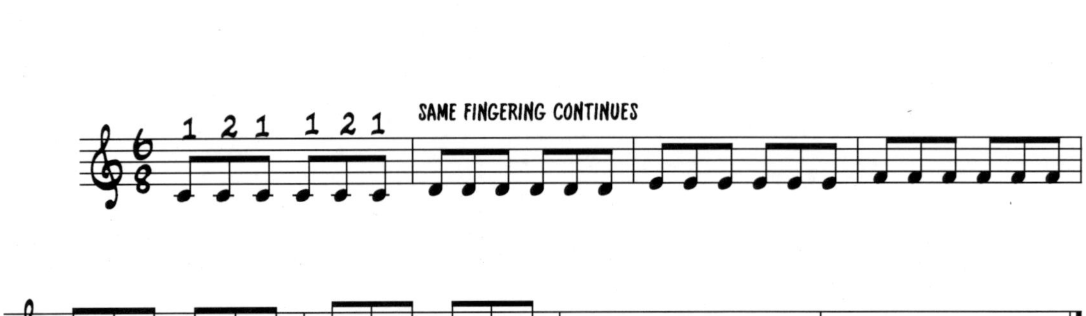

Ex. 8
Track 9

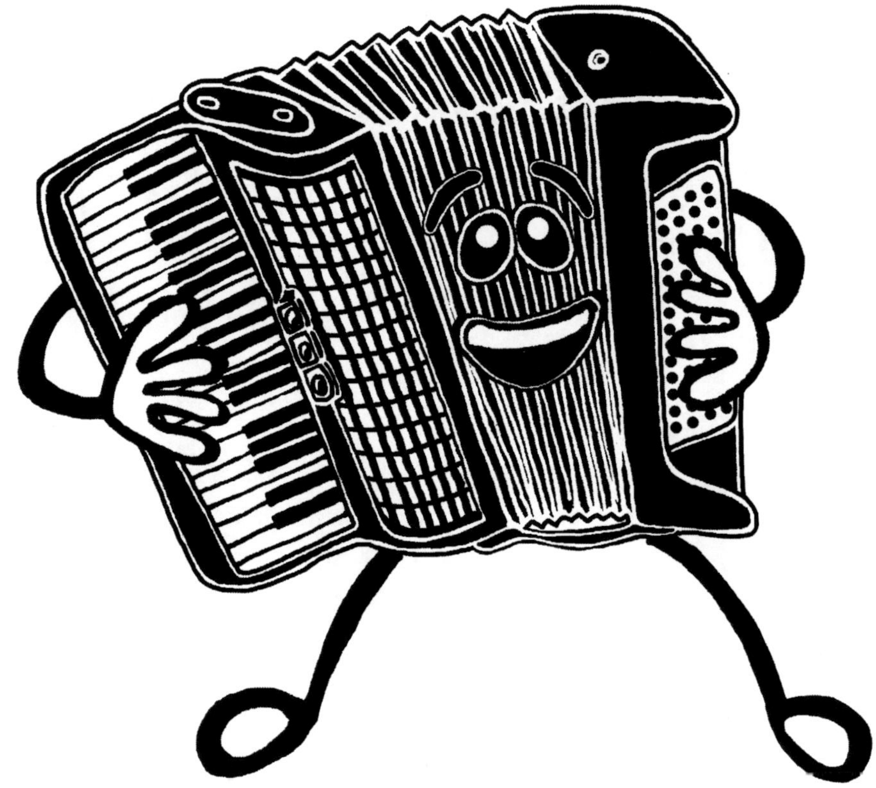

This page has been left blank to
avoid an awkward page turn.

Time to play a Jig!

Here is my composition from the start of the chapter.

The bass moves around with different chords. Spend some time really working on this so you can move from G to E minor and A minor to D7 in the 6/8 meter.

With the right hand, work on the 1-2-1 and the 3-1-3 alternation on the 2nd line. Also, watch the fingering on the last bar of the second line. It changes to the 1st finger on the repeat only.

Let's go!

Jig for John

Ex. 9
Track 10

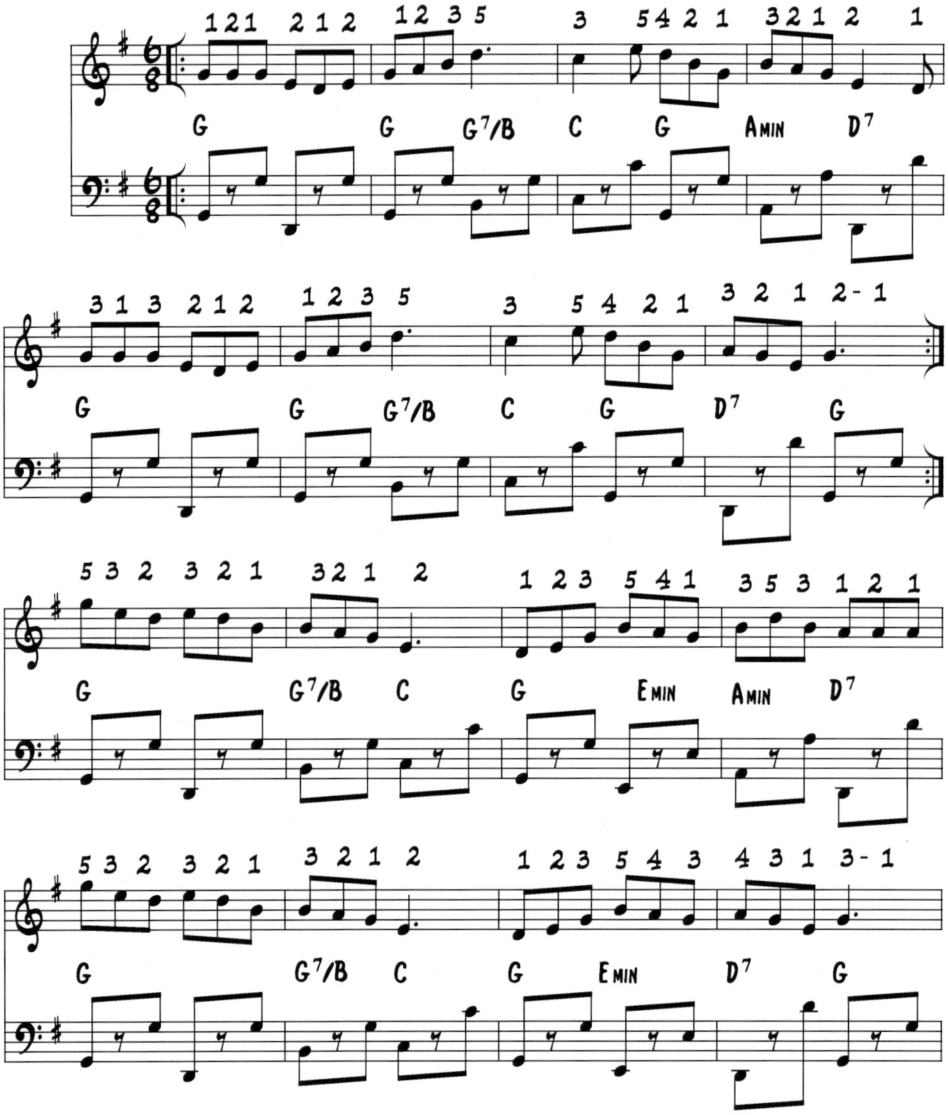

(Change to the 1st finger on the repeat.)

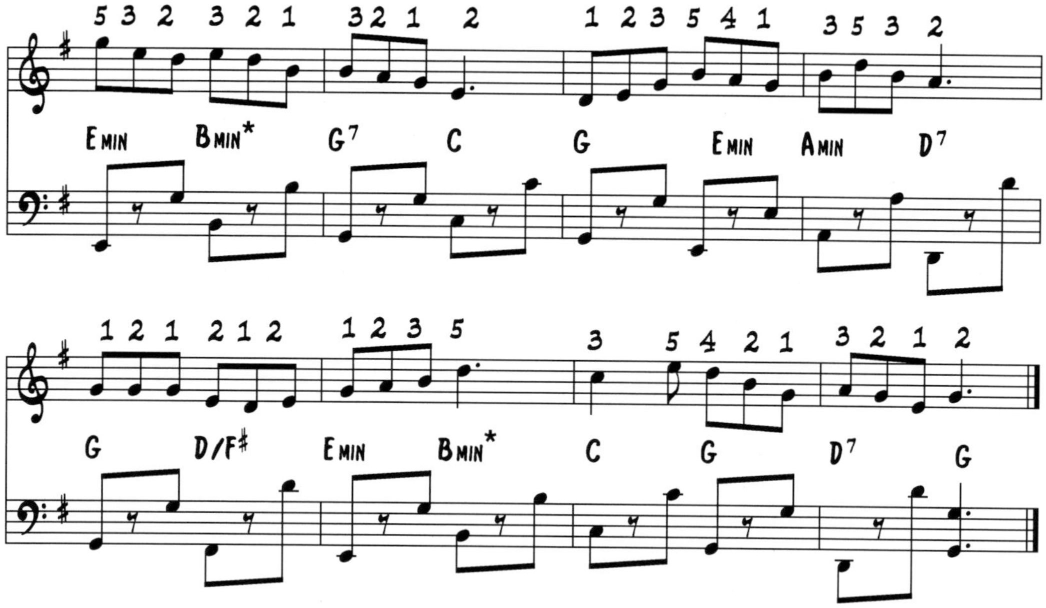

* Play G major if no B Minor available

Well Done!

Now that you have both hands playing and your jig rhythm is sounding great, you need to explore some other jig rhythms.

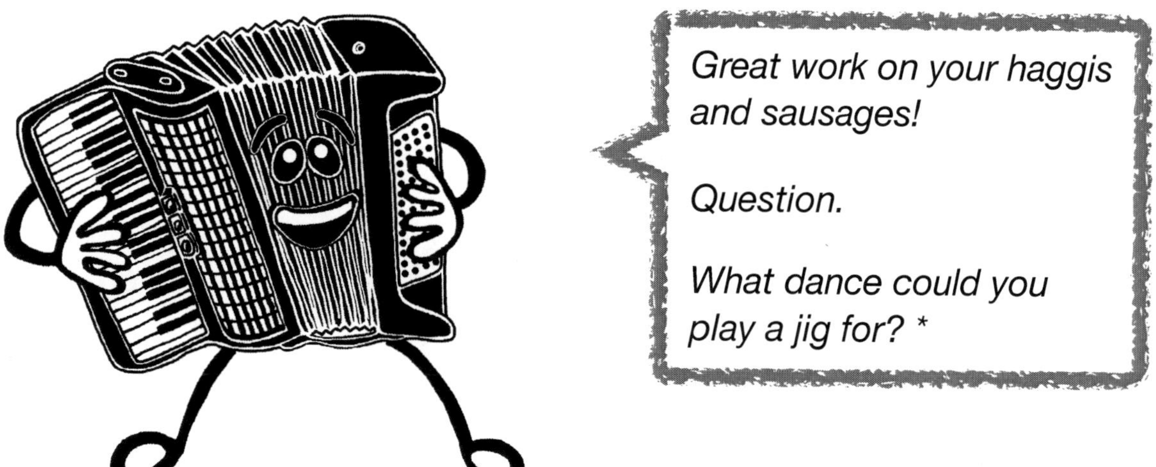

* Answer - Strip the Willow

More Jig Rhythms

There are variations on the basic 6/8 rhythm. To help you understand them, you are going to clap the next exercise. You can either count 1 to 6 or use our old friend, haggis and sausages.

In the first bar look at the placement of the dotted quaver (the first note). This would get one-and-a-half counts; the semi quaver that follows is in the gap or the "and" of 2.

The second bar has the same rhythm but reversed, with the semiquaver followed by the dotted quaver. The dotted quaver starts on the "and" of 1.

Practice these rhythms diligently away from your accordion, until you are comfortable with their placement. Once you feel confident, move on to the next exercise.

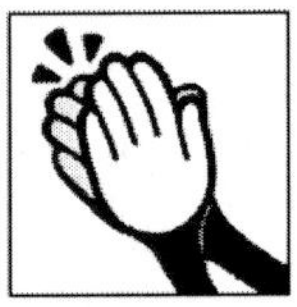

Ex. 10
Track 11

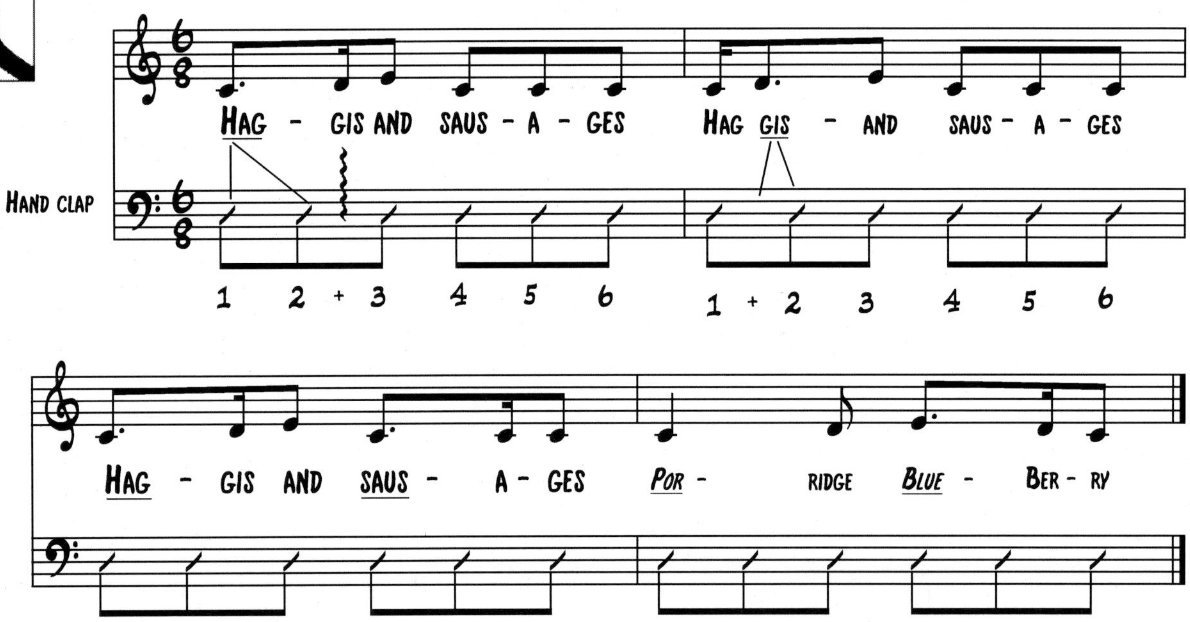

Below is a jig which has many of the rhythms you would expect to see in traditional music. From the previous exercises, you know how they fit with the 6 beats per bar.

It is time for you to add the left hand as well. Use the previous exercise to help you.

Remember to go slow and learn each hand separately. Keep counting too. This will really help with placing the notes, especially the dotted quavers and semiquavers.

Ex. 11

Track 12

Practice Tip!

Keep the right-hand notes as smooth (legato) as possible. Keep the left-hand notes nice and short.

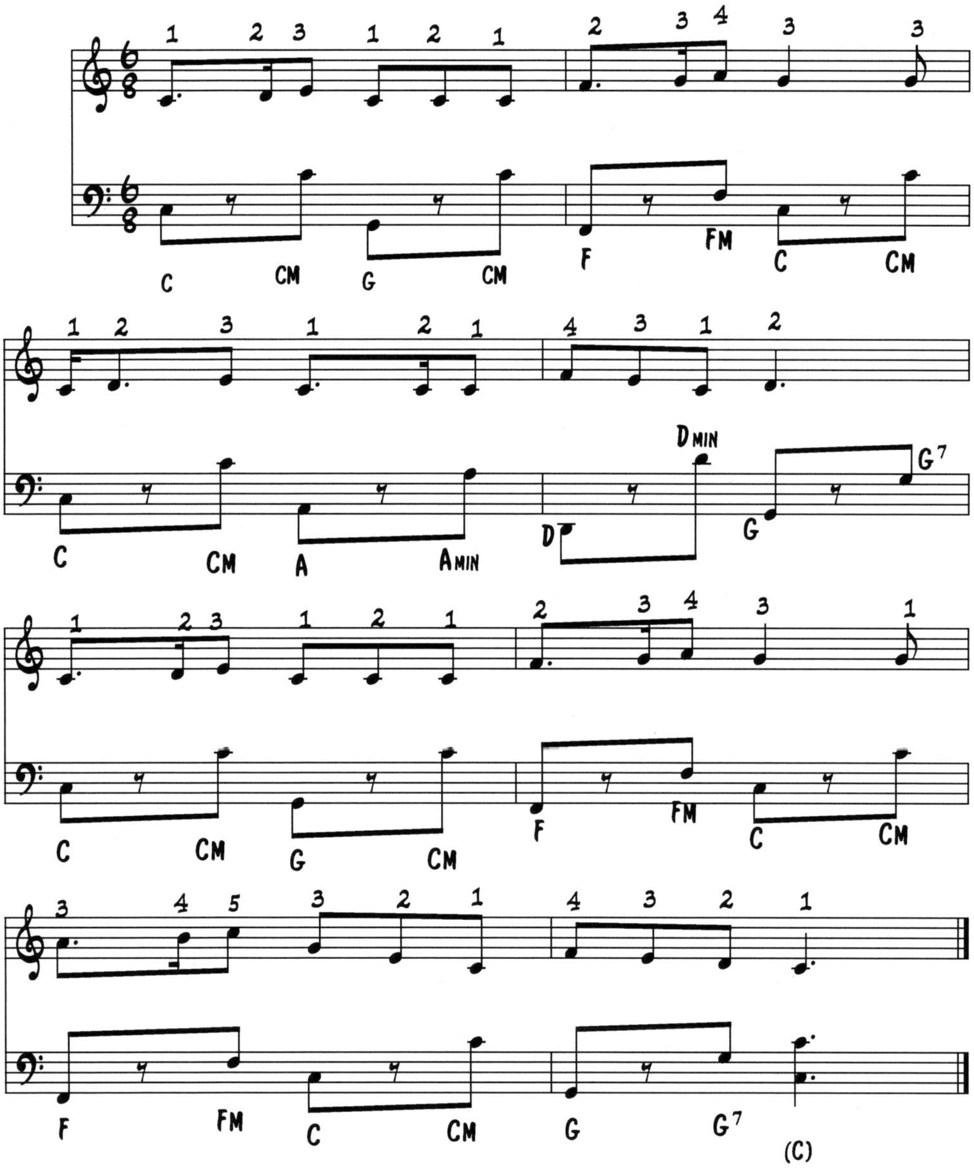

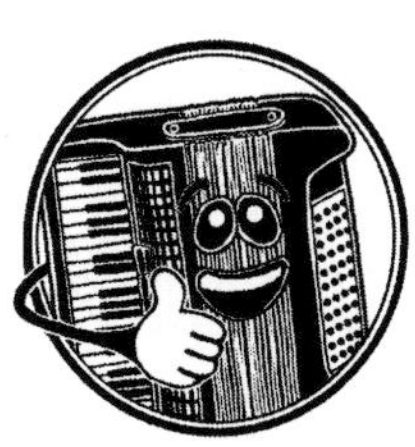

Well done!

You have completed the jig chapter.

Reels 4/4 C 2/4 or 2/2 ₵

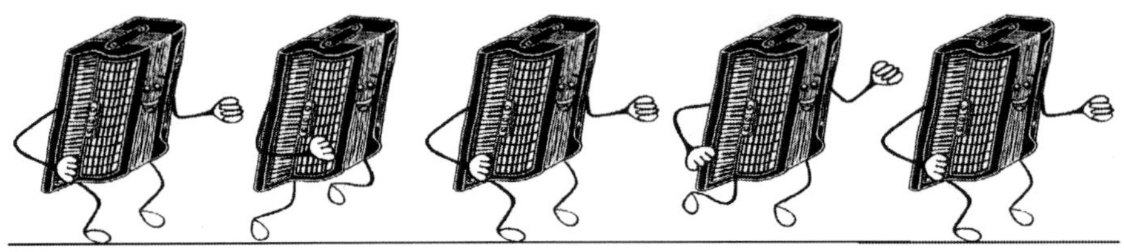

"Watermelon"

A reel has a running feel

What is a Reel?

It is a lively tune written in either 4/4 or 2/4.

The 4/4 time signature tells us there are 4 beats per measure and a crotchet gets one beat; 2/4 tells us there are 2 beats per bar and a crotchet gets one beat. You will learn more about both within the chapter.

If you say "watermelon" quickly a few times this will give you an idea of the reel rhythm.

Also, think of a running action. Go on, try both!

Let's look at a reel written in standard accordion notation as you might find it in a ceilidh or traditional music book. The chords can be found above or below the melody line.

The Forth Rail Bridge

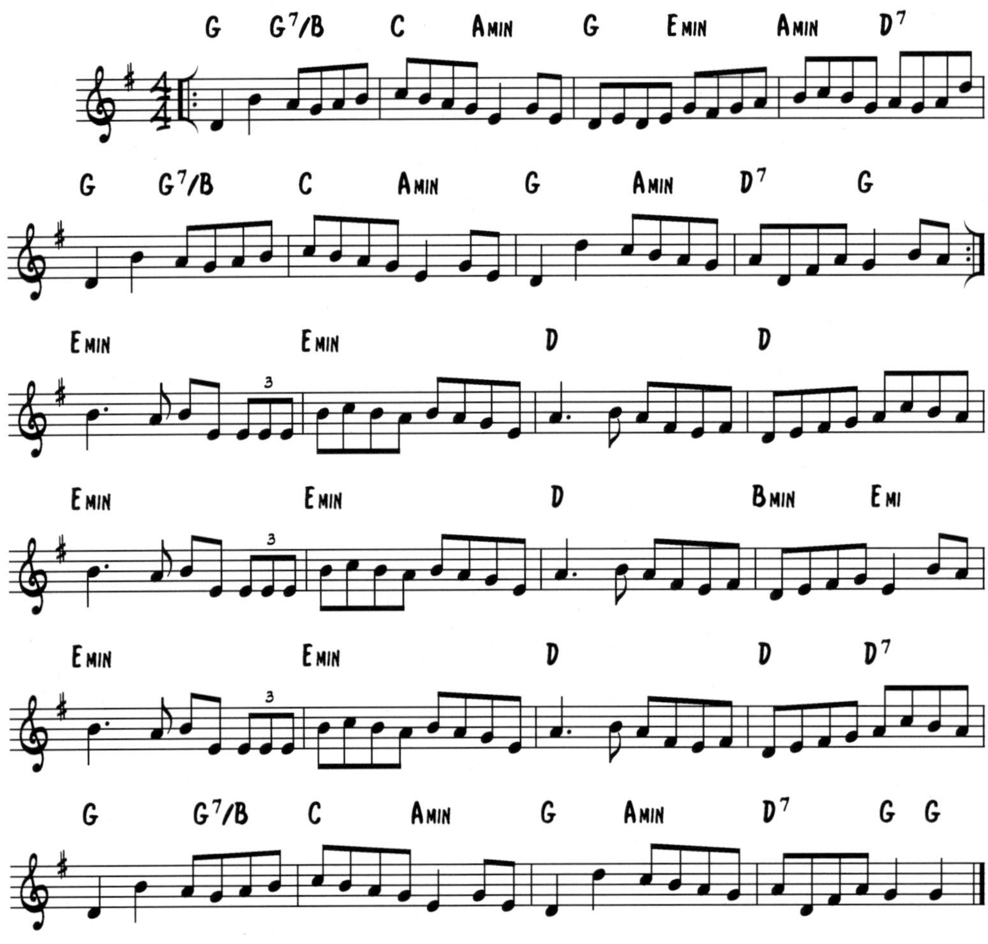

Playing the Left Hand in 4/4 Time

The first thing you need to do is learn how to play the bass in 4/4 time, then 2/4 time.

Let's look at the left hand of a reel you will learn later. It is in 4/4, so you will play bass notes on "strong" beats 1 and 3 and chords on "off" beats 2 and 4.

If you were tapping your foot or clapping, you would naturally tap or clap along with the tune on the strong beats. More on this later.

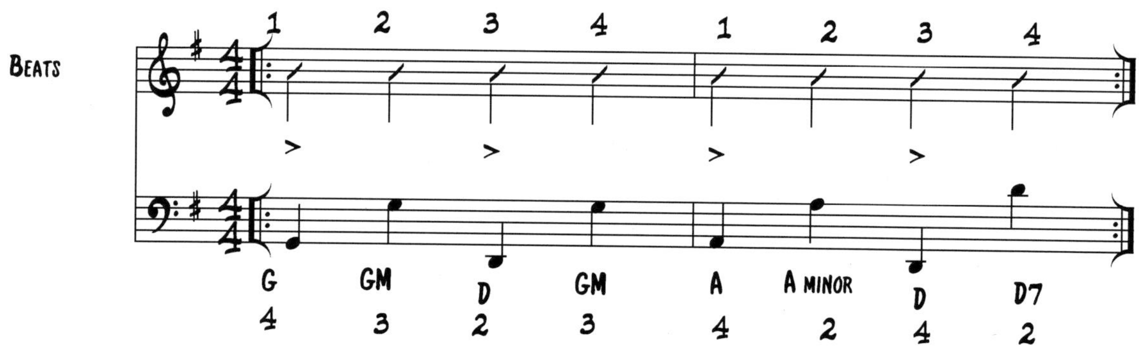

Below is the same exercise but the time signature has been changed to 2/4.

You will notice the bass is now written in quavers, but the feel is exactly the same.

In 4/4, use a fast 1-2-3-4 count; in 2/4, use a 1+ 2 + count.

The "2-in-the-bar" feel* is a practical way to think about 4/4 or 2/4 time.

It's time to try the bass for the reel. Have a look at Ex.1 on the next page.

* 2 strong beats per measure

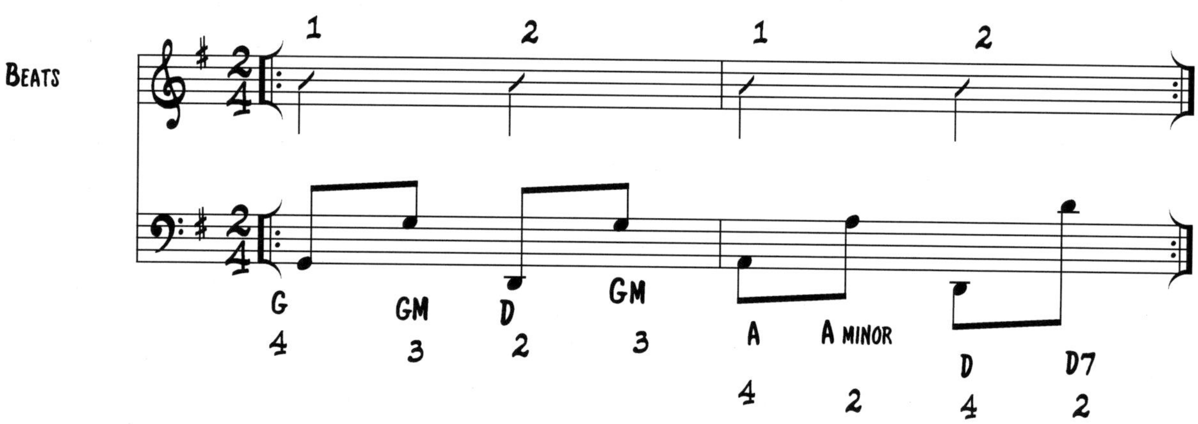

Ex. 1

Track 13

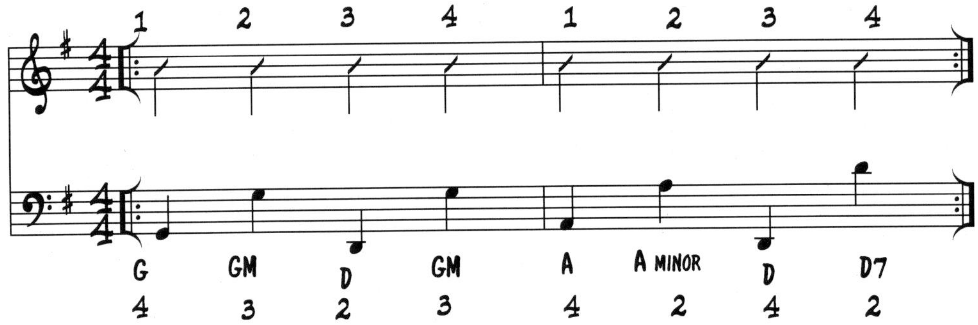

Start by finding G in the bass, one position up from C. Place your 4th finger on C, go directly up 1 floor in your lift (elevator) and get off at G, the 1st floor.

You then form your left-hand triangle shape when playing a full bar of the G major chord.

4th finger on G bass note
3rd finger on G major chord
2nd finger on D bass note
3rd finger back to G major chord

Bar 2 begins on A minor then goes to D7. Move up 2 positions from G. Play the A bass note with your 4th finger followed by the minor chord with your 2nd finger. Finally the 4th finger on the D bass note and 2nd finger on the D7 chord.

Repeat this exercise a few times until you are comfortable.

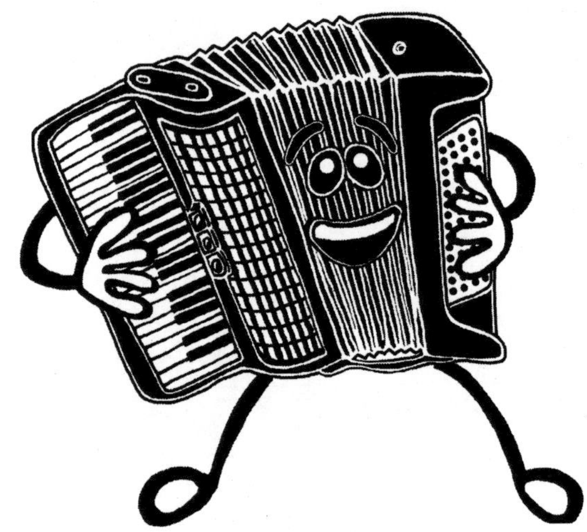

Let's Jump on that elevator to the 1st floor!

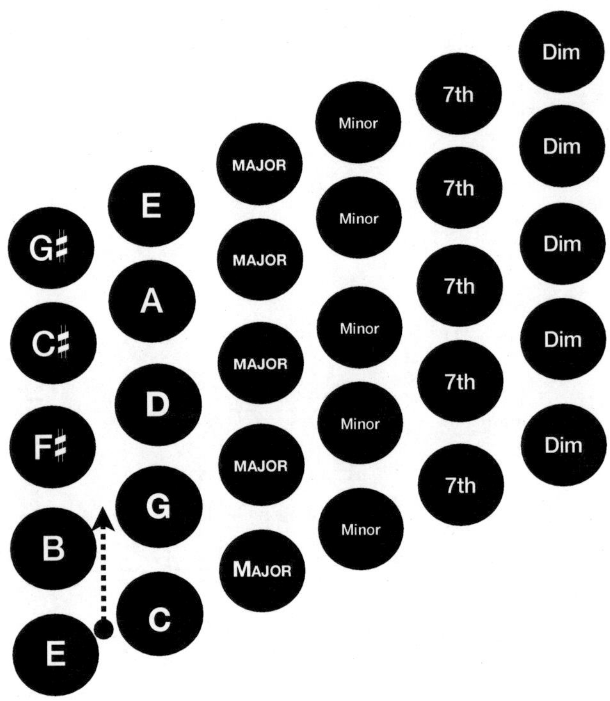

Metronome Practice

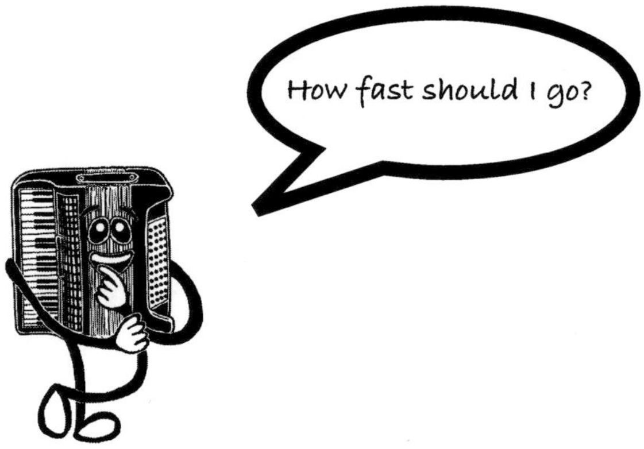

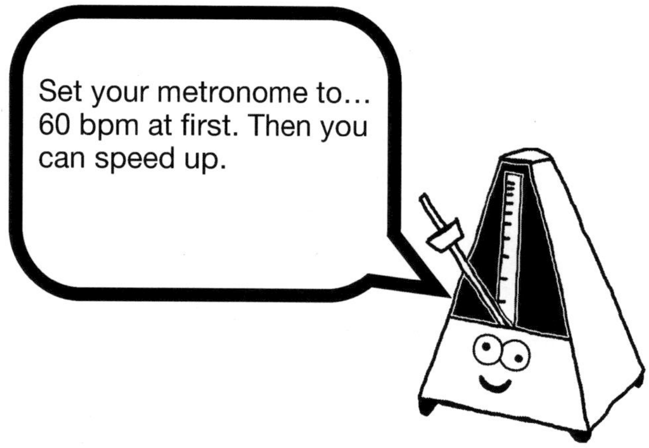

Reels can vary in speed from 100 bpm to 130 bpm.

When practicing the previous bass exercise, it is a good idea to set your metronome to 4/4 and 60 bpm. That way, you can play a bass note and chord to every click.

This is a great exercise as you won't rush playing the bass note or chord. Gradually increase the speed to 70 - 80 - 90.

Once you get comfortable and you are not fighting against the met onome, increase to 105 bpm and play the bass notes only on the clicks. The chord is in the gap.

The bass notes land on the strong beats, 1 and 3.

This highlights the 2-in-the-bar feel you need for reels. You will learn more about this in the right-hand section of this book.

When practicing the reels in this chapter, use the metronome to help with rhythm and time keeping.

Go back and try playing Exercise 1 (p. 24) with your metronome.

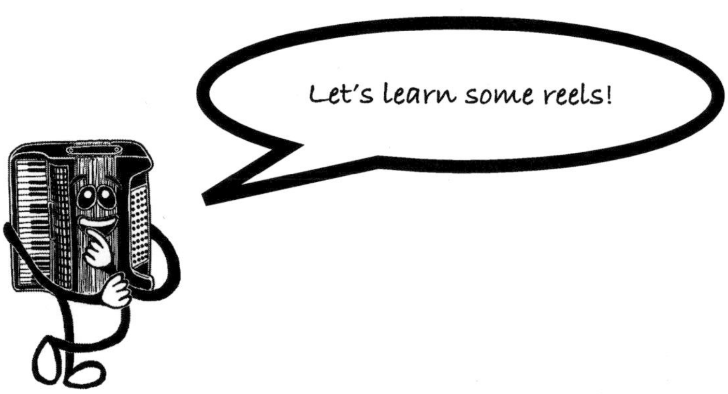

Simple Right-Hand Rhythms - Reels

Reels can be either written in either 4/4 or 2/4; within reels there are lots of quavers.

Let's do a clapping exercise to help with this characteristic. Use the word, "watermelon". The 4 syllables of wa-ter-mel-on fit nicely with 4 quavers.

Four steady claps replicate the 4 crotchet beats in the bar. On clap one say "water," on clap two "melon," clap three "water," and clap four "melon." This gives you the rhythm of the quavers against which the left hand would be playing.

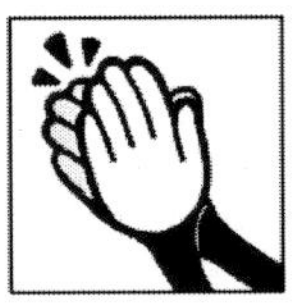

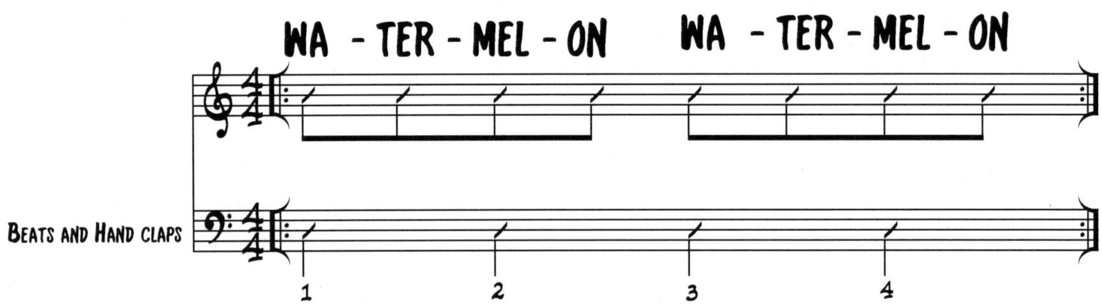

Ex. 2
Track 14

The feel of the reel is actually in 2. With the bass exercise in Ex. 1 (p. 24) the main emphasis is on beats 1 and 3.

Let's try Ex. 2 again, this time with your metronome. You might find sheet music where the suggested tempo for a reel is 112 bpm. That is 112 beats per minute for a crotchet.

Clap along with every beat and say "water-melon" again. What do you think of the speed? It's too slow for a reel.

This time, double the speed on your metronome to 224 BPM and try Ex 2 again. Clap every beat and say "water-melon" to match the quaver feel.

It becomes a tongue twister but it's much closer to the desired speed of a reel; counting at 224 bpm, however, is a drain on our brain power.

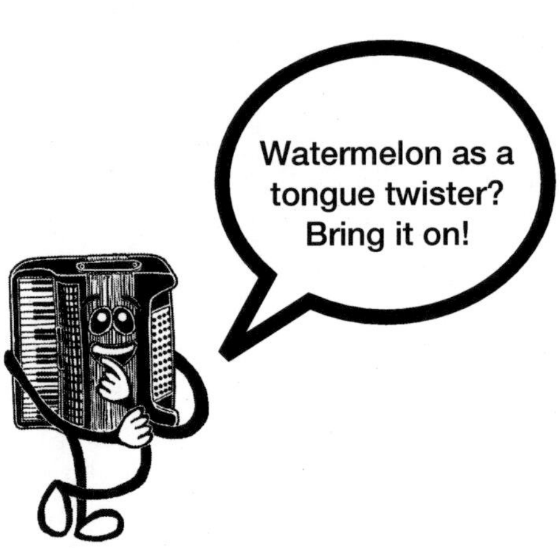

So, what do we do?

The answer is on the next page!

Let's try Ex. 3 and switch your metronome to 2/4.

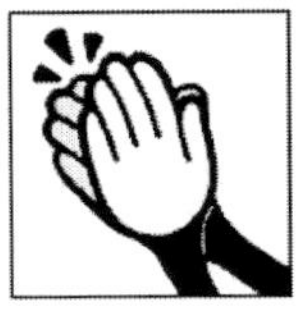

On every click, clap your hands and say "watermelon."

This creates yet another tongue twister, but this is a perfect exercise as it produces the correct 2-beats-per-bar feel.

Ex. 3
Track 15

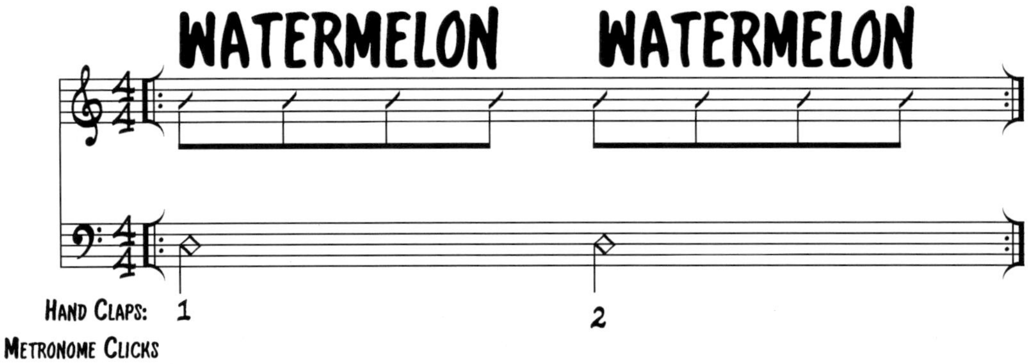

When you clap your hands along with the metronome click, this is where you would play the bass note. The chord would be in the gaps or the "off" beat.

When reading and learning reels in 4/4, count the quavers "1+2+3+4+" so you know exactly where they go.

Reels are notated in several different time signatures.

The common ones are 4/4, 2/4 and 2/2. All have a 2-in-the-bar feel. In 4/4 the strong beats in the bar are 1 and 3. In 2/4, the strong beats are 1 and 2 but they are written differently.

It is important to understand the differences and how to apply them to your playing.

4/4 is also know as *common time* and and is notated with a 𝄴

2/2 time is also known as *cut time* and indicated by a 𝄵

The "C" does not actually mean "common time" as common time originated in 3 and comes from the Holy Trinity. It used to be notated as a full circle. The incomplete circle would mean *not* perfect time. With time, the 4/4 measure came to be recognized as common time as most popular music appeared in this time signature.

The 2/2 signature is indicated with a C with a line through it. In 2/2 time, the top number tells you there are 2 beats in the bar; the bottom number tells you that a half note get one of those beats.

Let's look at different examples of all these rhythms.

The next few exercises sound exactly the same; however, they are all written in different time signatures. It is important that you know the difference.

Below is 1 bar in 4/4 with the pulse on beats 1 and 3.

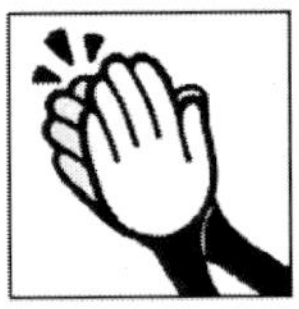

Ex. 4

Track 16

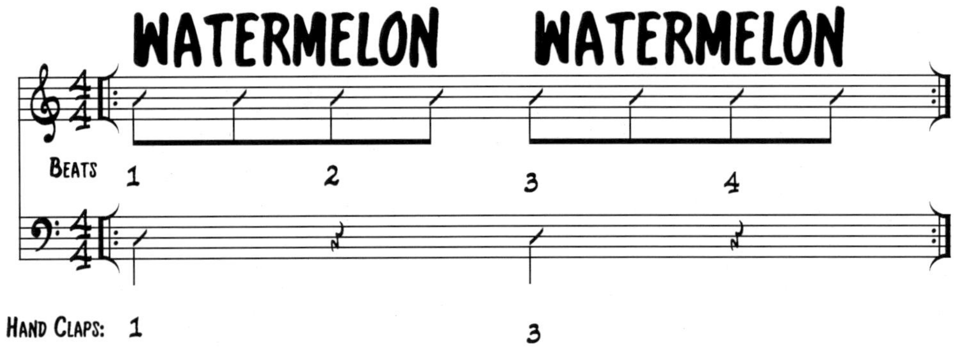

The next example is exactly the same as above; this time, the C indicates "common time" – 4/4.

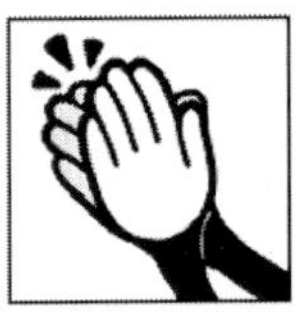

Ex. 5

Track 17

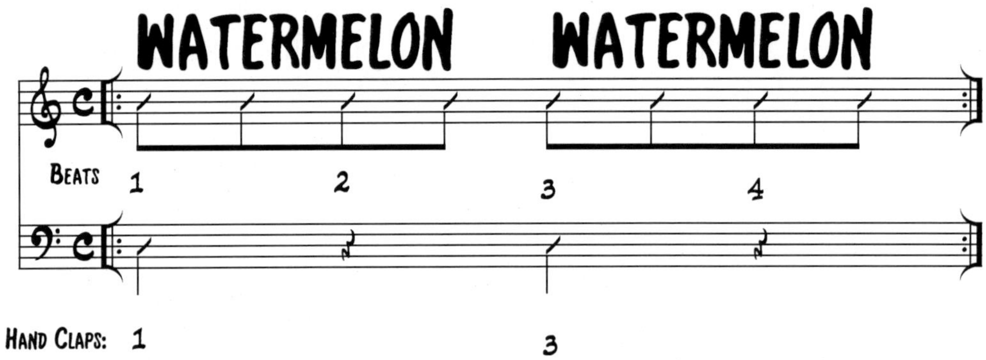

Next there is an example in 2/2. Notice how this looks the same as 4/4.

However, it is important to note the time signature has changed and the minim would be the same as the crotchet beat in 4/4.

For example, when you clap this one, the pulse is on 1 and 2, but the "watermelon" sounds exactly the same, as do the quavers.

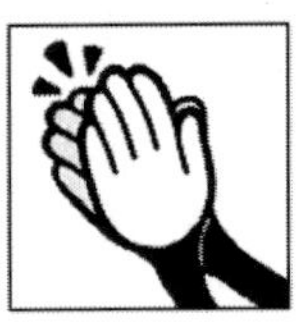

Ex. 6

Track 18

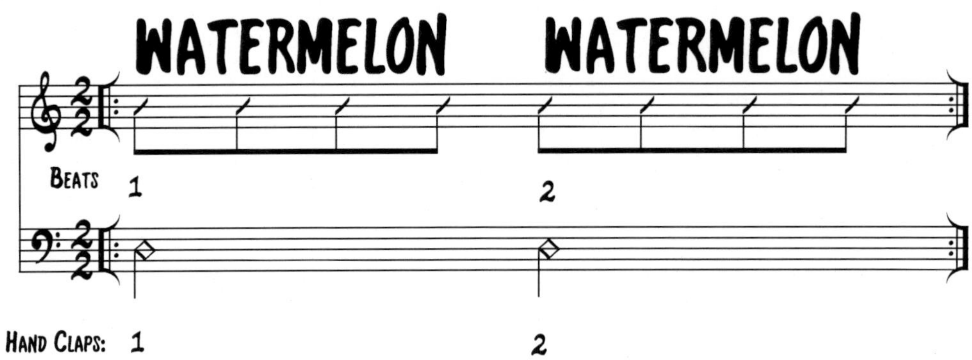

Ex. 7 below sounds just the same as Ex. 6, but notice the time notation is a C with a line through it instead of the 2/2. Both are used to signify "cut common" or simply "cut time".

Historically, a lot of composers wrote reels this way, it was very common. As music progressed and 4/4 became much more in the mainstream, cut time became slightly outdated. It is still argued to this day which way reels should be notated. More often than not, modern composers will write in 4/4 or 2/4 for reels.

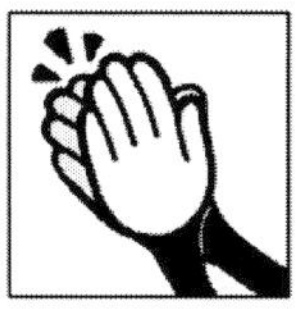

Ex. 7
Track 19

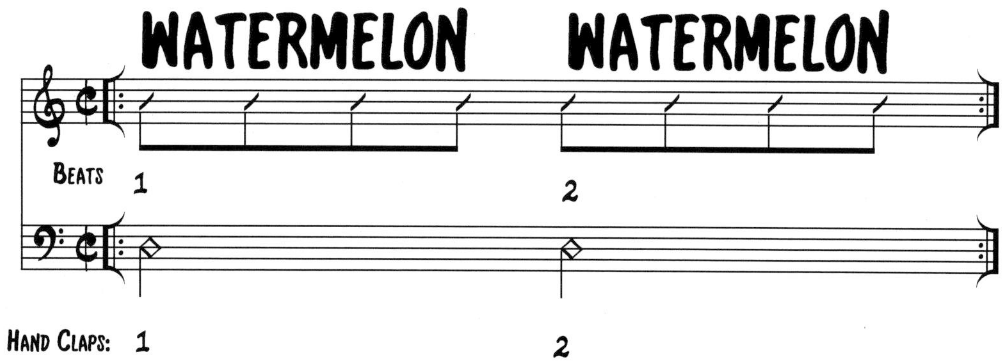

The final example of the "watermelon" challenge is written in 2/4. Again, it's very common in reels. You will see the use of semiquavers. When writing in 4, you tend not to see semiquavers as some people argue it is easier to read and play quavers.

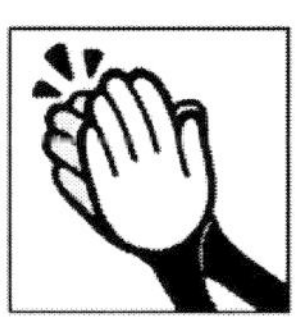

Ex. 8
Track 20

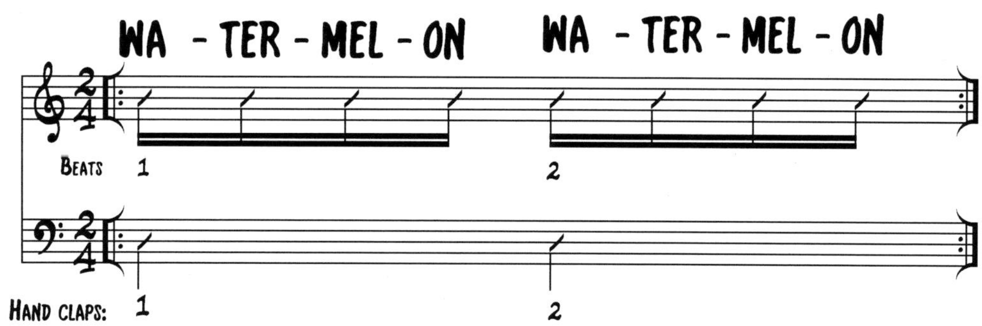

With all these examples of how reels can be written it is important to know how to play them with both hands.

Each of these examples sounds exactly the same, but is written differently. Remember the 2-in-the-bar feel of every example.

How do we play with both hands at once?

Let's learn your first reel with the quaver feel you have learned from previous exercises. This one is in 4/4 time.

Learn it slowly and keep the quavers even, especially in the 2nd bar where you cross over with the 3rd finger.

Ex. 9a
Track 21

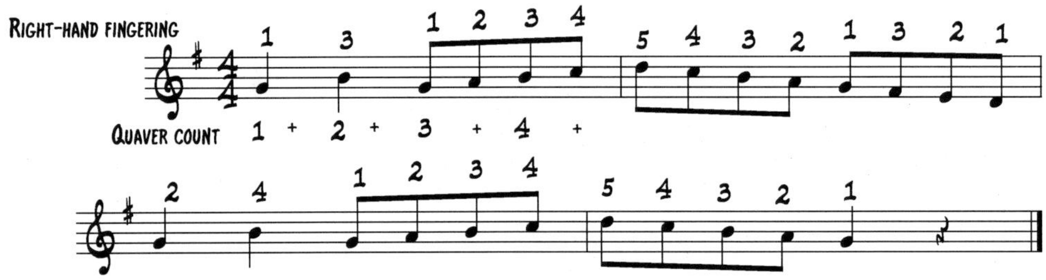

Below is the left-hand part for this first reel. Learn this before moving on to the next exercise. Go nice and slow and be consistent in your sound.

Ex. 9b
Track 22

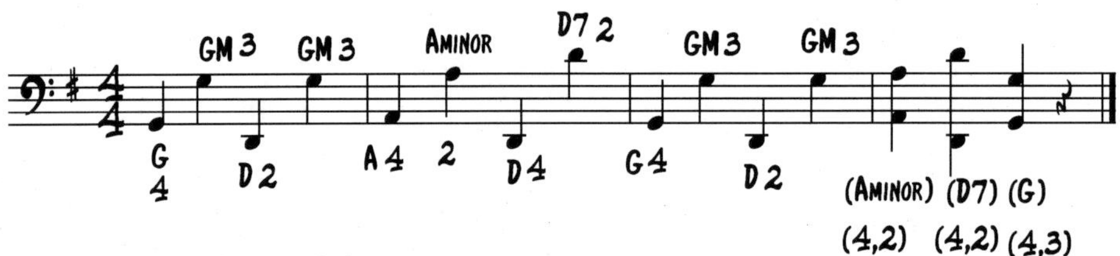

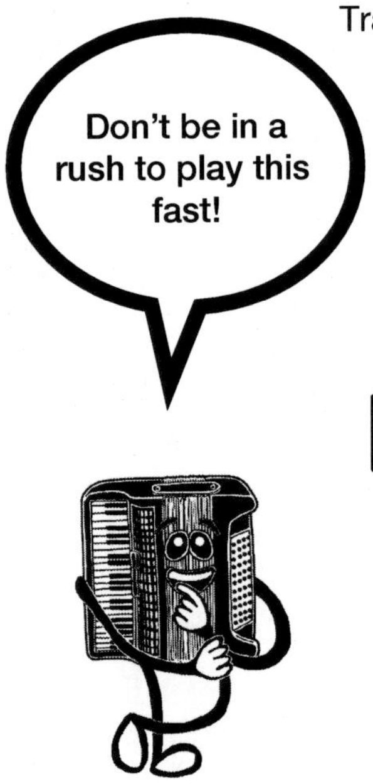

Are you ready for both hands at once?

Keep the right hand smooth, especially when playing the quavers. Focus on keeping the left-hand notes crisp and short.

Ex. 9c
Track 23

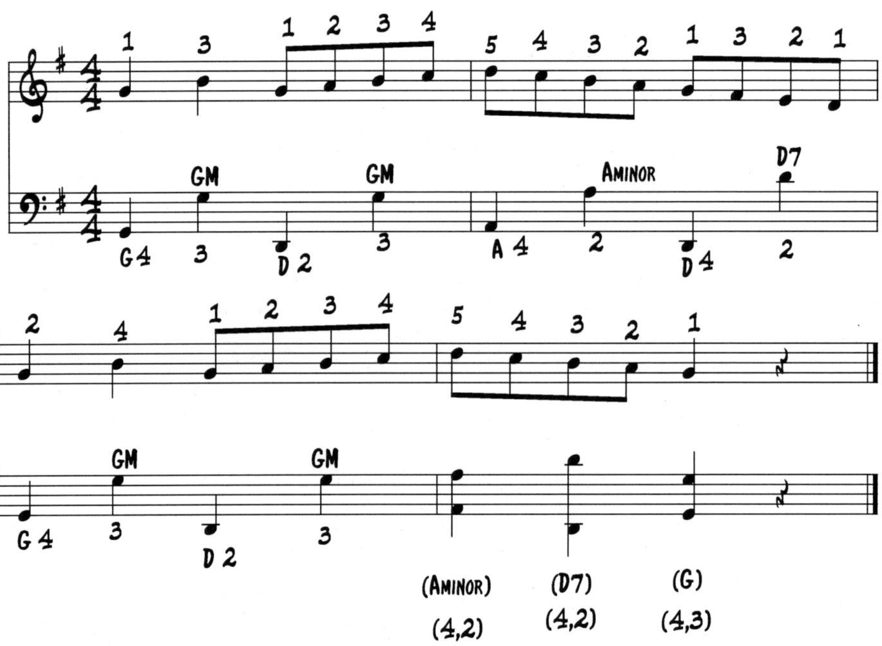

Well done on your first reel in 4/4! In the tune below, you are going to learn a reel in 2/4.

In time, you will know how to play both hands when you find tunes yourself.

Learn the right hand of the melody. Remember you now have 2 crotchet beats per bar.

You can sub-divide them into quavers by counting 1 + 2 +.

Within the first bar there are 2 quavers followed by 4 semiquavers. You can count this as "1 + 2-it-is-a."

Ex. 10
Track 24

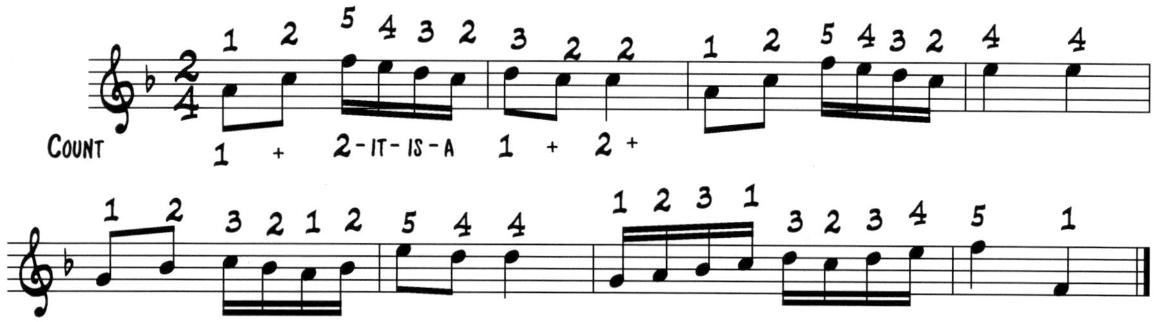

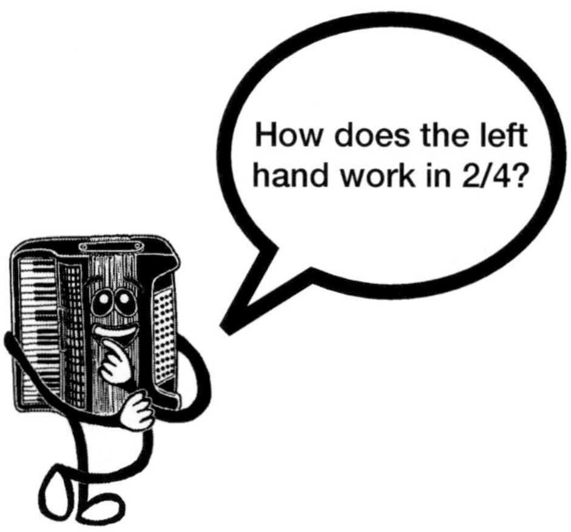

The left hand in 2/4 is in quavers. Within every bar you will find 4 of them. You can count them with "1 + 2 +".

Generally, the pattern will be: bass note, chord, bass note, and chord.

Sometimes, with quick chord changes you might find the bass and chord played simultaneously.

Below is the left-hand pattern for the reel you have learned above. The bars without written bass notes or chords are exactly the same as the previous bar.

Ex. 10b
Track 25

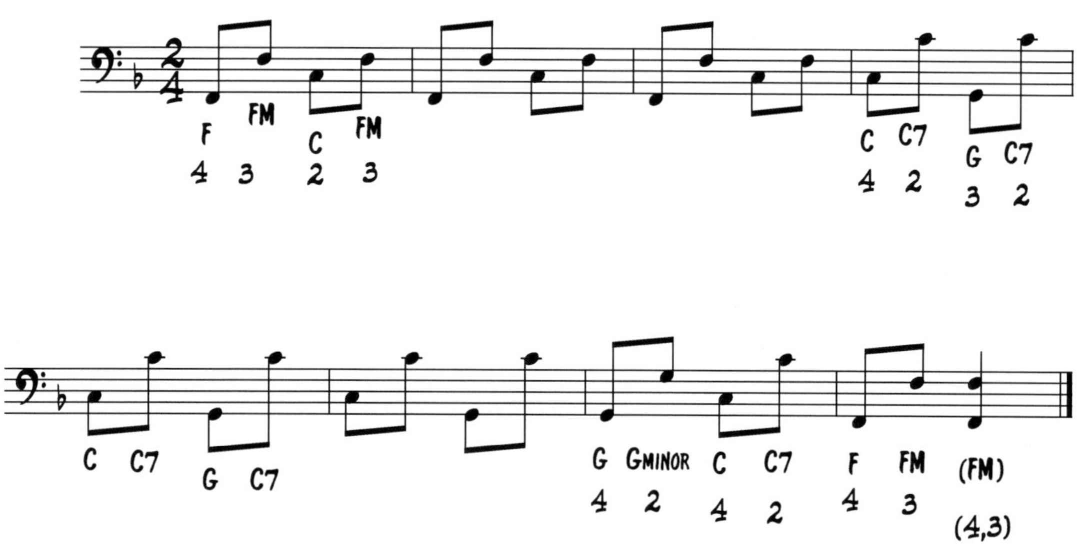

Things to look for in 2/4

In the right hand, the first bar starts with 2 quavers. This is matched in the bass by playing an F bass note then an F chord.

The second half of the bar has 4 semiquavers with 2 semiquavers going with each bass, as you can see with the lines, matching the left and right hand together.

Focus on practicing this figure and go slow. Keep the right hand held down and keep the bass and chords nice and short. Think in terms of passing one melody note to the other; this will help when adding both hands together.

There is a tendency when using both hands for the right hand to copy the left, or vice versa. Go super slow and build up hand independence.

Practice Tip - When you play the first note with both hands (super, super slow) the thumb of the right hand coincides with the 4th finger of the left hand. The right hand stays down and the left hand shoots back up. Keep using this technique for the entire tune.

Continue to work on both hands together. Think of playing this as a slow air initially, then gradually build up speed. When you feel confident and have learned it, try it at "reel" speed. Remember the 2-in-the-bar feel.

Ex. 11
Track 26

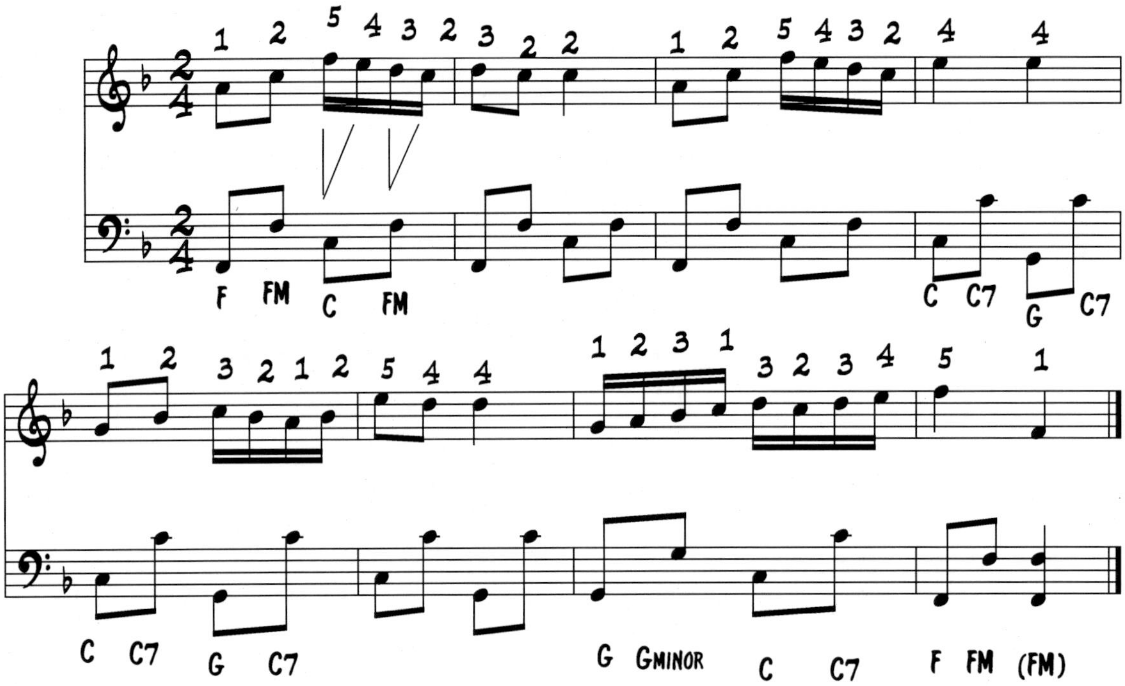

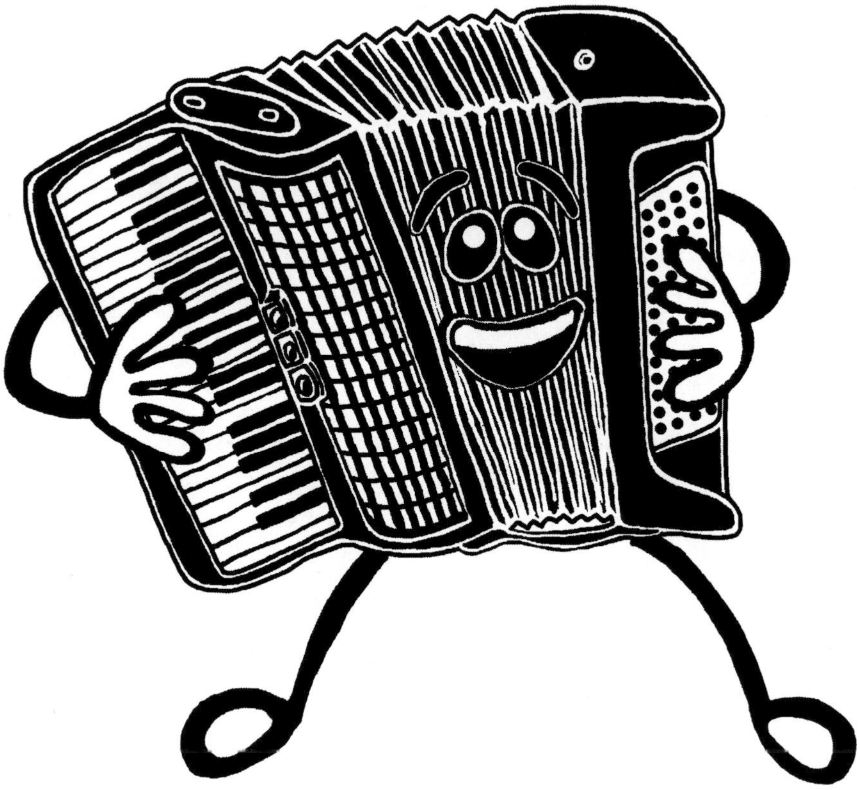

This page has been left blank to
avoid an awkward page turn.

Right-Hand Techniques

There can be lots of repeated notes within Scottish traditional music.

Below shows a typical example of how the repeating note would look in a reel.

How would you play these?

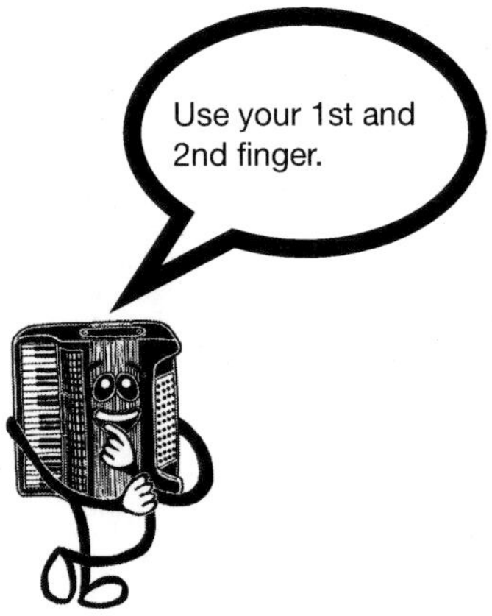

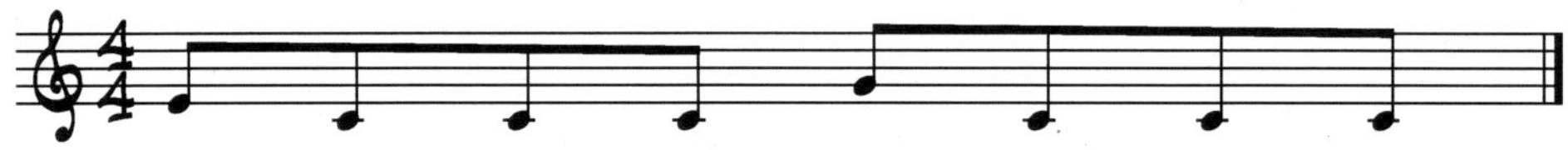

To make the repeated notes sound smooth and close together, use your 1st and 2nd finger on the same note.

Look at the exercise below. Use the accordion keyboard mechanism to help you. The idea is to not let the key come all the way back up before using your 2nd finger to play the next C. Think of your 2nd finger on a spring action as it fires in to replace the 1st finger.

The same applies when replacing the 2nd finger. Try to avoid gaps between the notes. The quaver rests help break up the C's for you.

Go slow and really focus on your finger action, catching the key before it comes back up entirely.

Repeat this exercise many times and make it part of your practice routine. You can build on this and play a C major scale using the 1-2-1 technique.

Ex. 12

Track 27

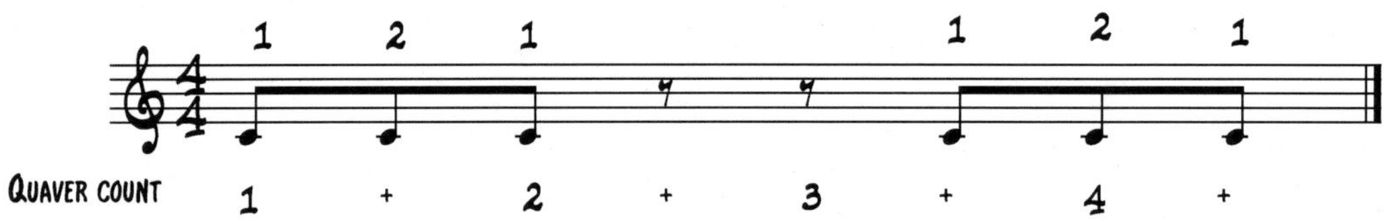

In Ex. 13 below, you'll find a typical example of how the repeating note would look in a reel.

Work on the right hand first, then slowly add the left.

Remember to keep the right hand legato (smooth) and the left hand staccato (short).

Ex. 13

Track 28

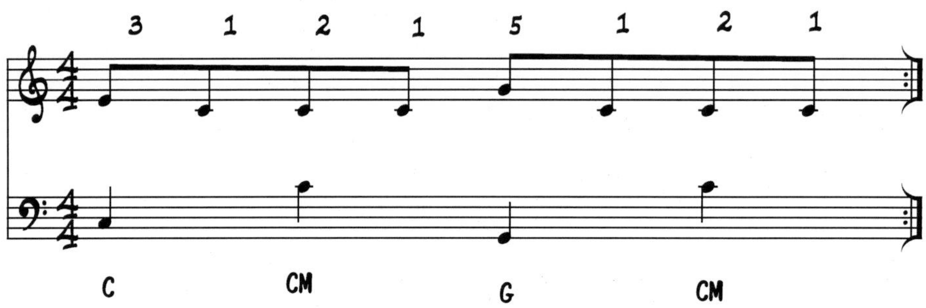

In addition to frequent quavers, triplets often appear in reels.

A very common technique is to repeat the same note with a triplet, sometimes with a quaver to start the process. This would be four strikes of the same note played in quick succession.

This can be tricky, but with practice you will get it. As you can see in the example below, the thumb is on middle C, then you play your 3rd and 2nd finger and back to your thumb.

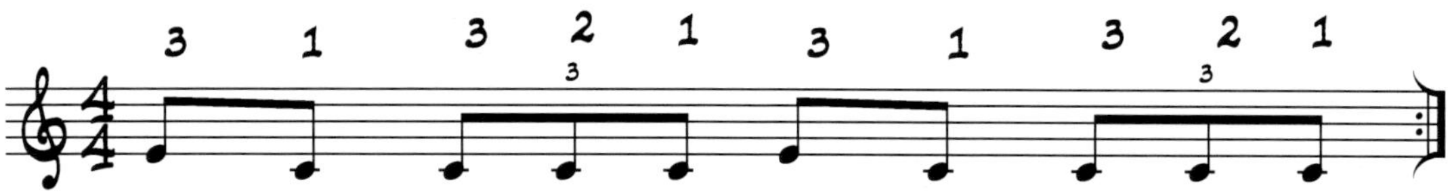

Ex. 14
Track 29

In the exercise below, you can practice the triplet over the C major scale.

First – do it with just the right hand. When you feel comfortable and have gained confidence, try it with both hands at once.

Pay attention to the triplet coinciding with the bass chord. Make sure the bass and the right hand match perfectly.

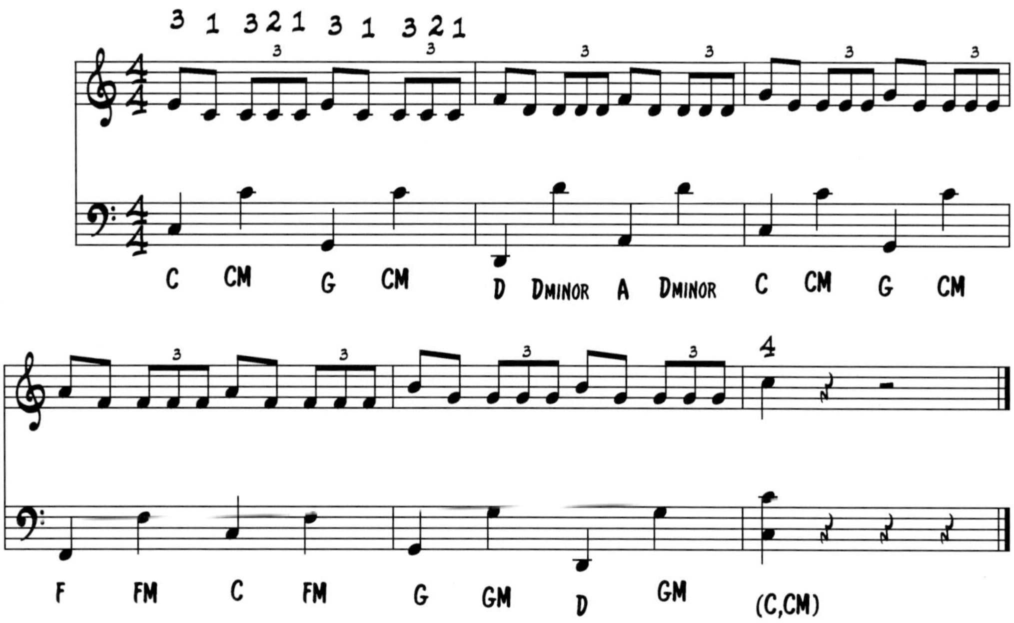

Ex. 15
Track 30

Another common technique is to approach the triplet from below. In this instance you would use your 2nd finger first, then play the triplet with the 3-2-1 fingering.

Practice this with both hands separately and slowly before playing both together.

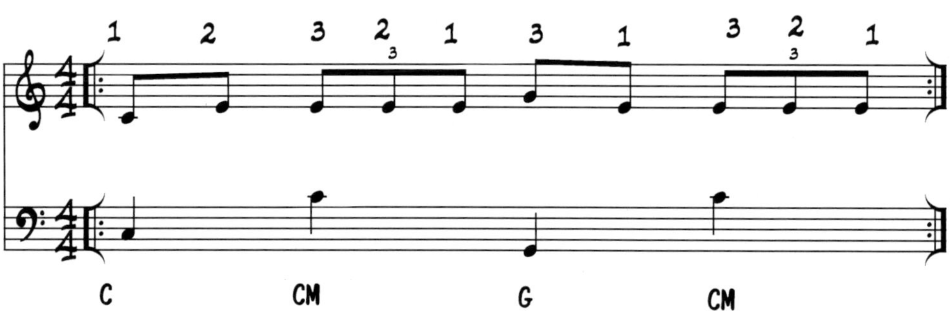

Ex. 16
Track 31

Time to Play Reels

Below is the reel from the start of the chapter. Learn each hand separately and then bring them together one bar at a time.

Work on the triplets and get them as smooth as possible within their allocated time.

Remember to use your metronome to practice these 2 reels. It is really helpful in keeping you in time and not speeding up.

The Forth Rail Bridge

Ex. 17

Track 32

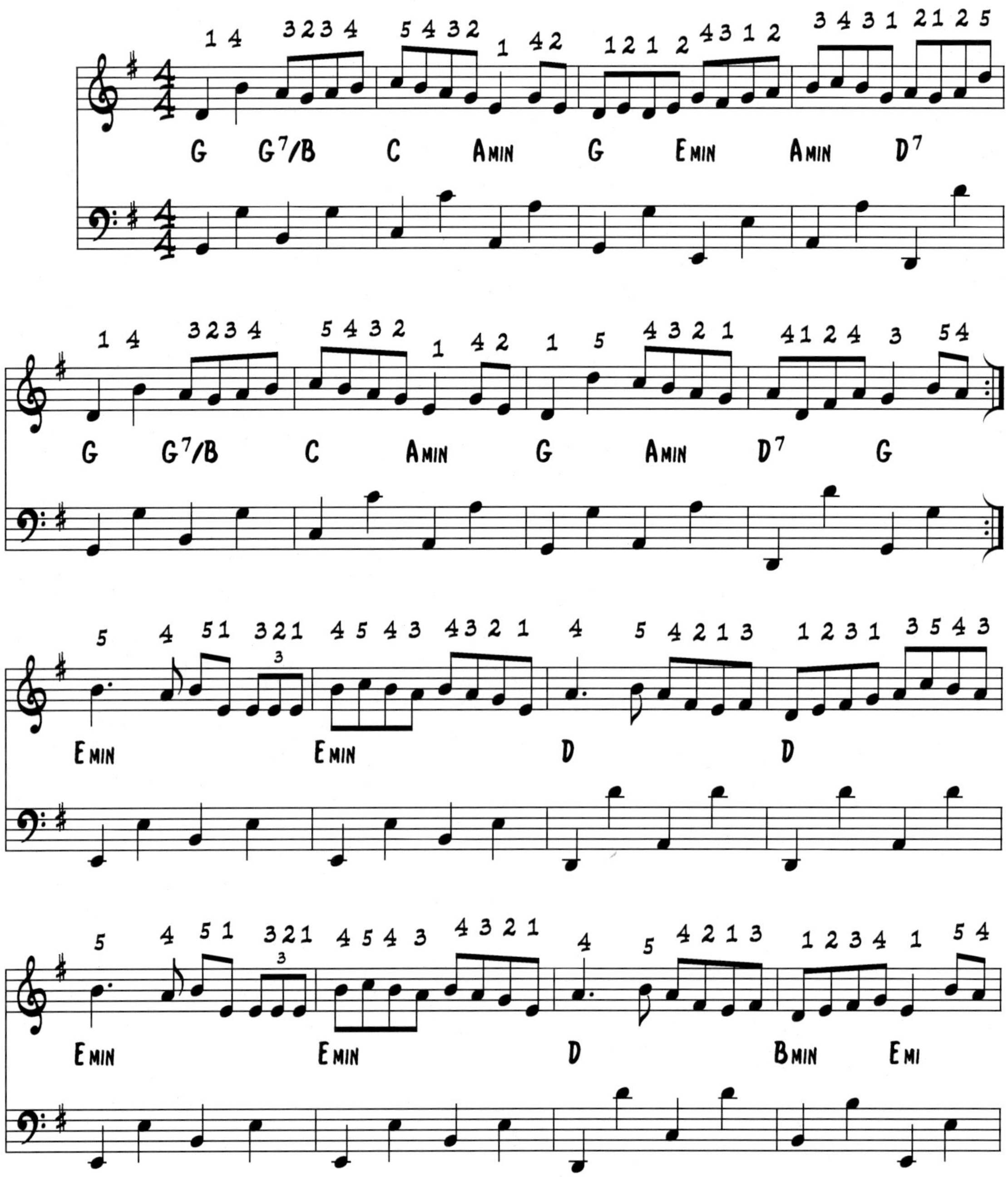

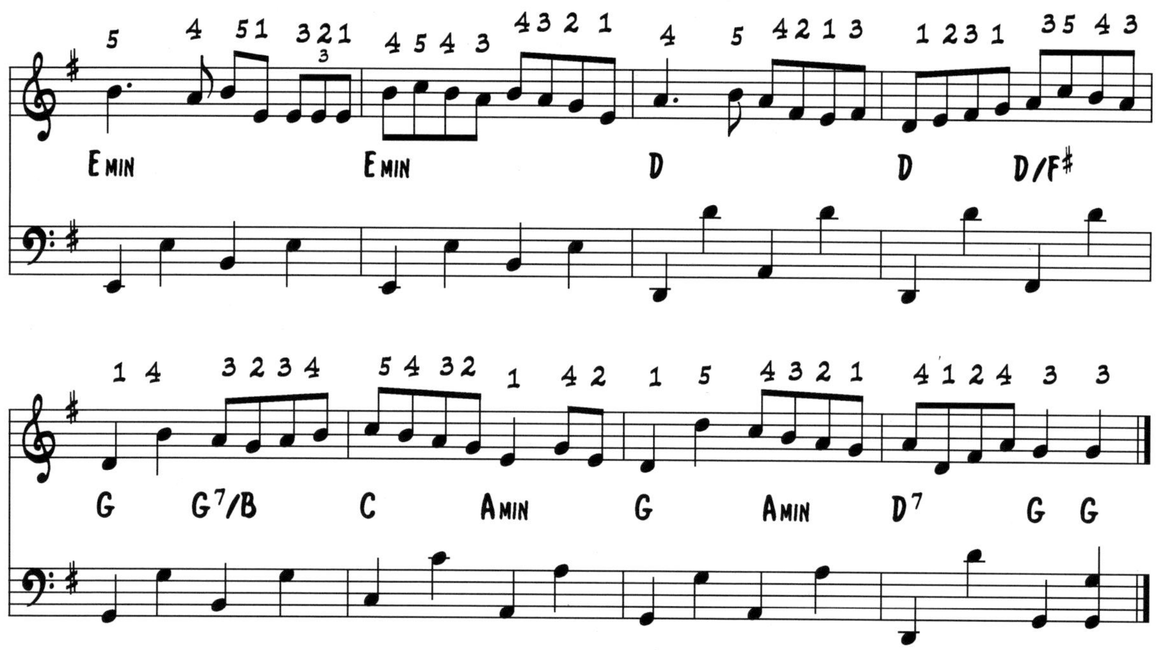

The last tune in this chapter is “The Morning Loop”

Always examine the tune first before you tackle it.

Key Questions

What is the time signature?

What is the key signature?

Are there any notes, rhythms or chords you are unsure of? If so, examine them closely and work them out before diving in.

Can you sing the tune in your head and understand it?

Let’s look at the next tune and spot things to highlight.

There is use of the 1-2-1 finger exercise you learned earlier, just like the triplets in the previous tune.

The second bar has some finger crossing with 1-2-1-2.

There are some dotted crotchets so be sure to place the following quaver in the gap.

Watch out for the quaver triplets again.

Ex. 18

Track 33

The Morning Loop

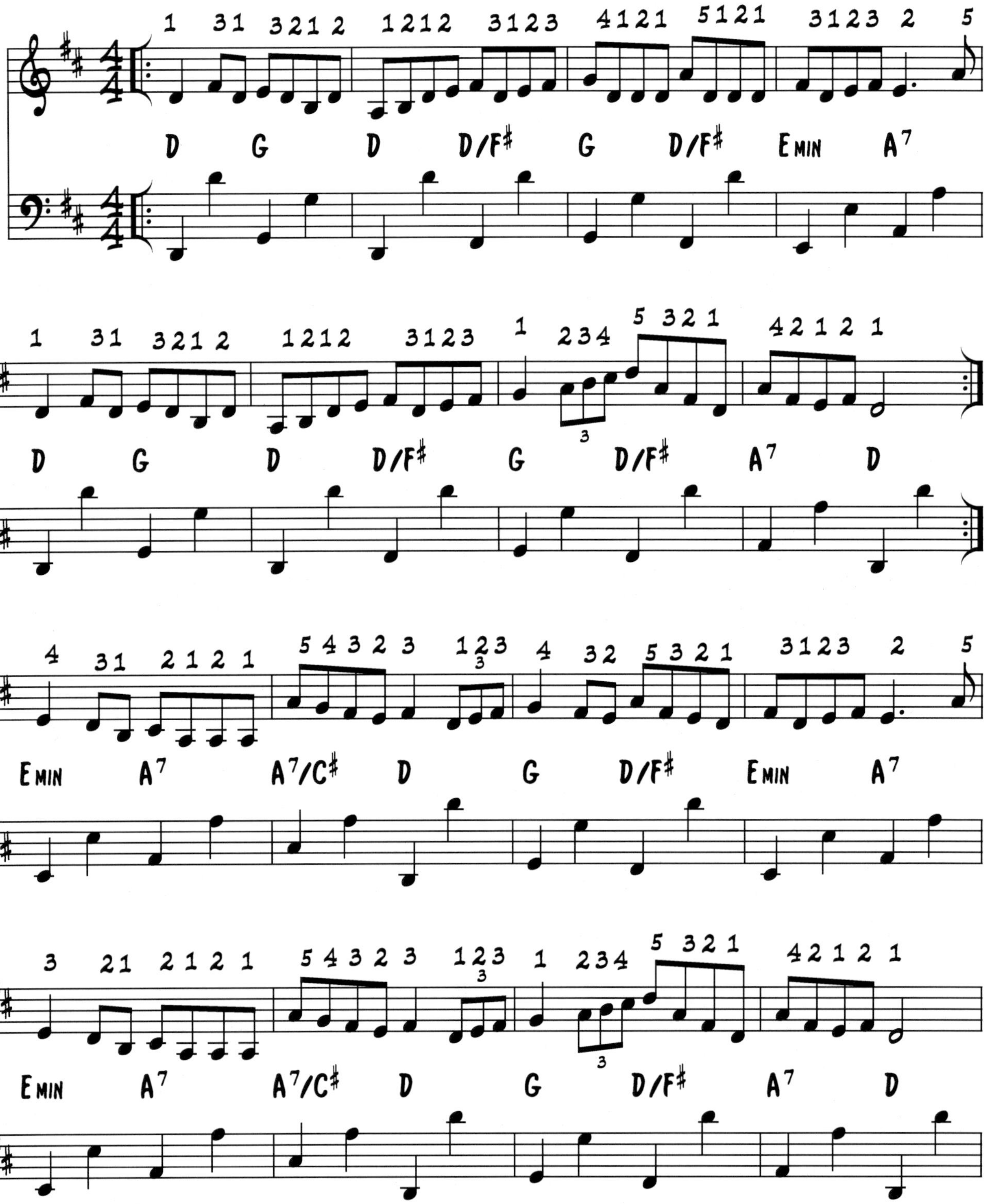

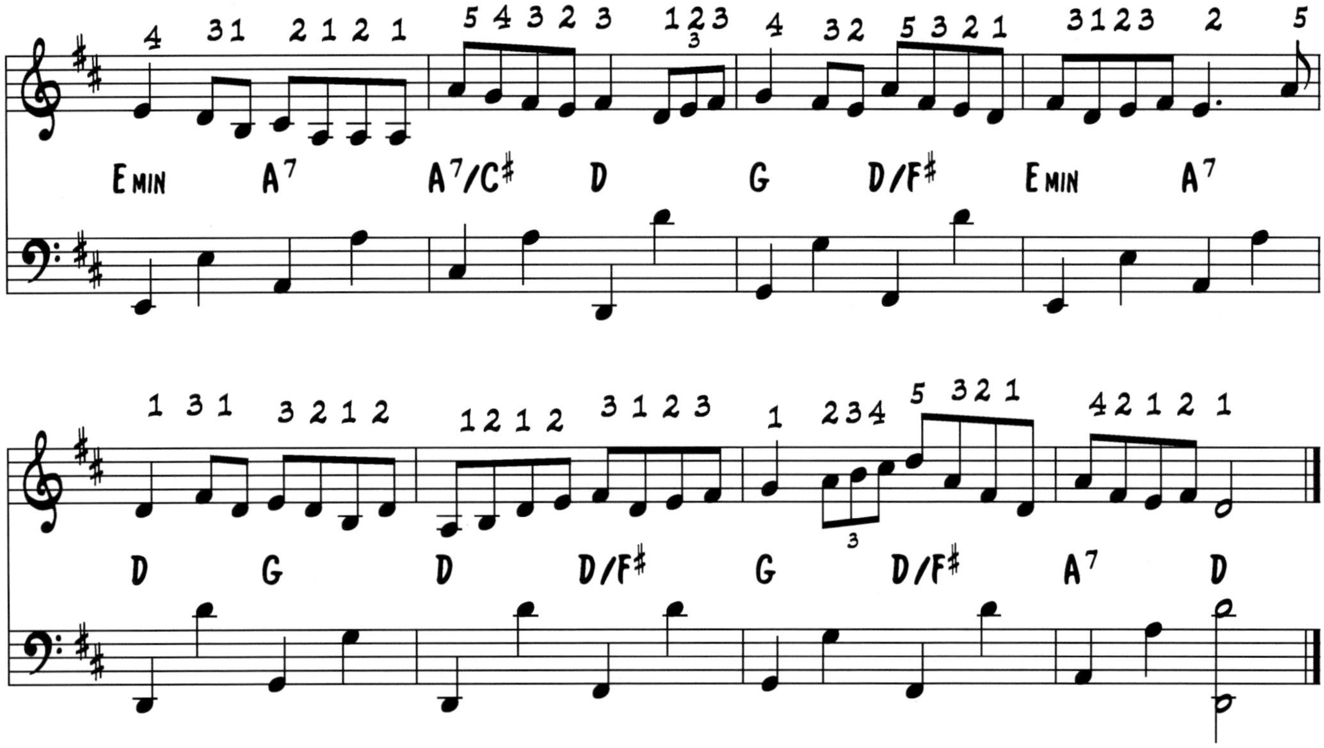
EMIN A7 A7/C# D G D/F# EMIN A7
D G D D/F# G D/F# A7 D

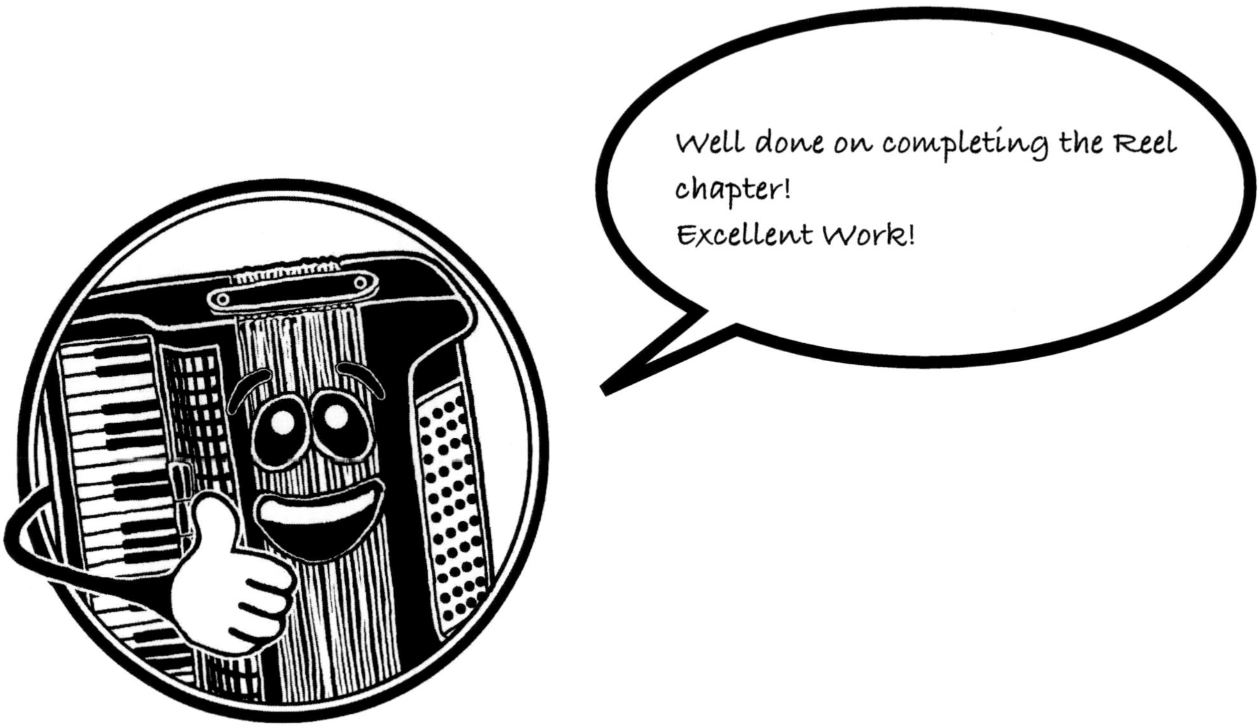
Well done on completing the Reel chapter!
Excellent Work!

Strathspeys

"Chicken's Feet"

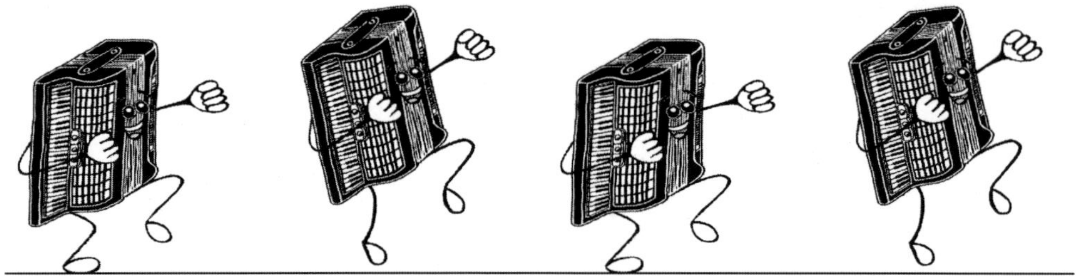

A traditional strathspey has a hopping feel. Let's go!

What is a Strathspey?

A strathspey is a dance rhythm written in 4/4 and played quite steadily.

It features frequent use of the "scotch snap" rhythmic figure, where a short note is followed by a longer note; for example, a semiquaver followed by a dotted quaver.

If you say the phrase "chicken's feet" it will give you an idea of the strathspey rhythm.

Or, think of hopping on one leg. The 'jumpy' feel is what you are after.

Let's look at a strathspey written out in the standard accordion notation you might find in a ceilidh or traditional music book.

Lachlan's Bounce

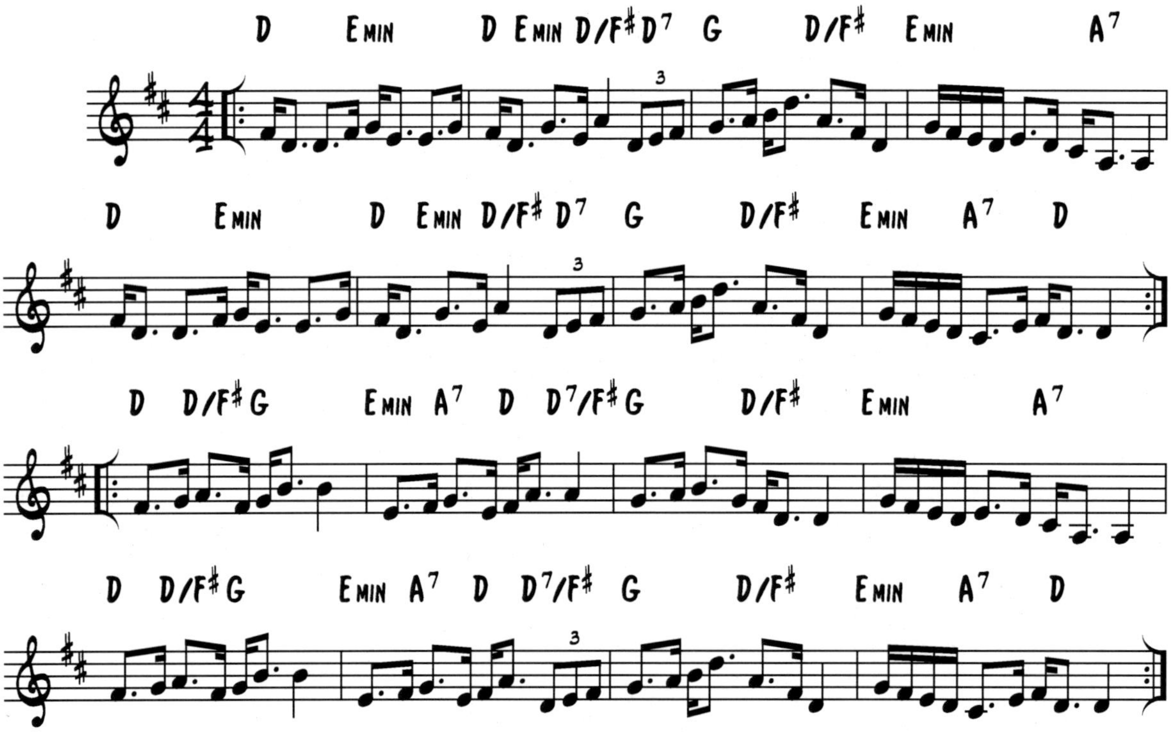

How to Play the Left Hand

The first thing we need to do is learn how to play the basses in a strathspey.

As mentioned previously, it is in 4/4 time. With quick chord changes to fit the melody, you often have to play the bass note and chord together.

Check the bass example below in the first two bars of "Lachlan's Bounce".

Ex. 1

Track 34

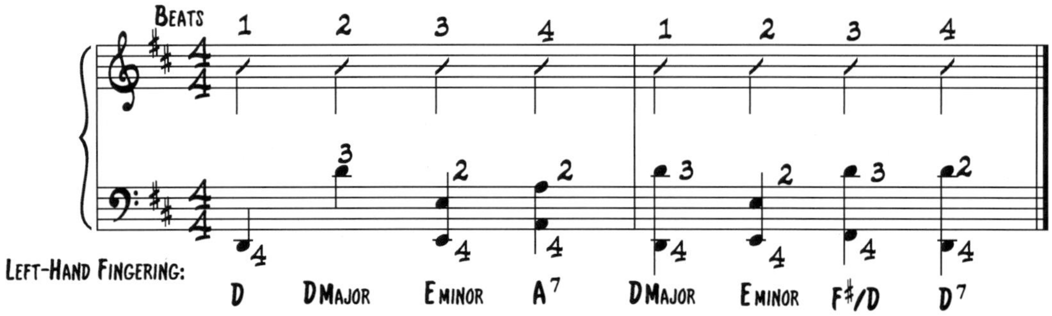

Start by finding D in the bass, 2 positions up from C. Place your 4th finger on C and imagine it is in a lift (elevator) that goes straight up to the second floor. That is where you get off. You have arrived at D. Look at the diagram for assistance.

The next chord is an E minor. You will have to jump in your elevator and go up 2 floors. Most accordions will have E marked in the bass for a reference point. This makes it much easier to find.

Play the E bass note and E minor chord together in the space of 1 beat. The A7 chord is one floor below E. Drop down and move your 2nd finger out to the 7th chord. Practice the first bar until you are confident in moving between chords.

The second bar has the bass and chords playing together for each beat. Watch out for beat 3 as the bass changes to an F♯ located just behind D.

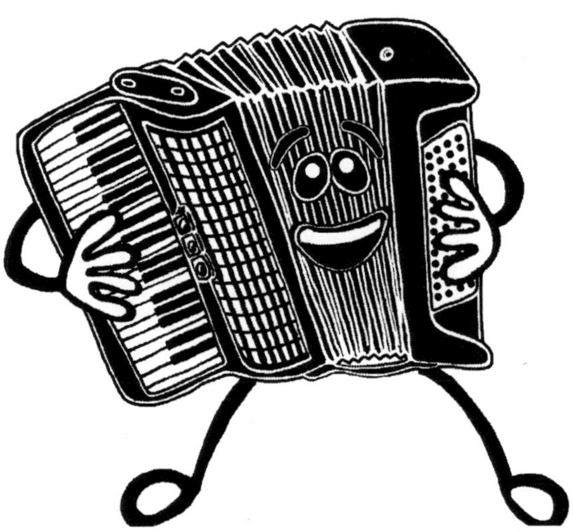

Let's jump on that elevator to the 2nd floor.

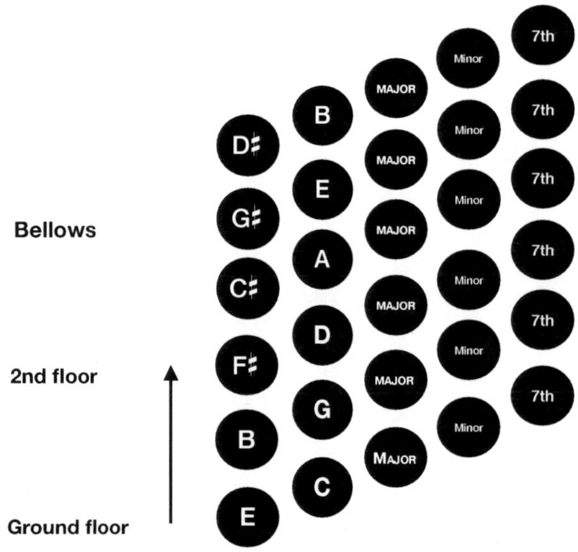

Metronome Practice

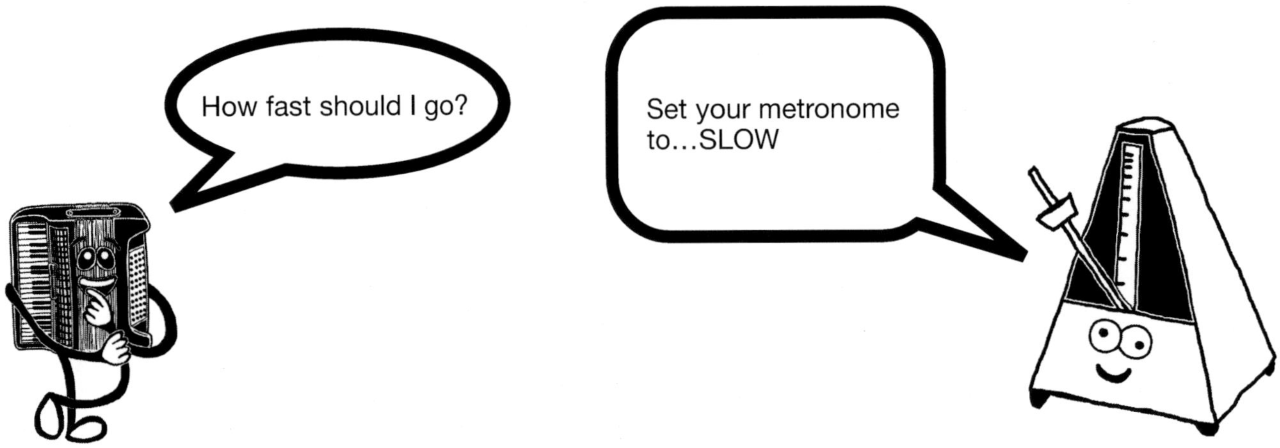

When practicing this bass exercise, it is a good idea to set your digital metronome to 4/4 and crotchet = 50 bpm. That way, you can play the bass and chords on clicks 1-2-3 and 4.

This is a great exercise as you won't rush playing the bass note or chord. Gradually increase the speed.

When comfortable and no longer fighting the metronome, change the speed of the metronome to a performance speed of 105 bpm to 110 bpm.

Gradually increase the speed so you are comfortable with landing the bass and chords on the click.

Bass notes sound on beats 1 and 3, chords are played on beats 2 and 4.

Practice **without** the metronome, slowly until you feel confident with the movement, particularly when playing bass and chords together with the jumps. Start at the slowest speed and work at it.

To practice the strathspeys in this chapter, use the metronome to help you with the rhythm, especially when you add both hands together with the scotch snaps.

As always – GO SLOW!

Simple Right-Hand Rhythms- Strathspeys

Within strathspeys, there are often a lot of “scotch snaps” in which a short note is followed by a long note.

Let’s try a short clapping exercise. The phrase, “chicken’s feet,” will help you understand the rhythm a little easier.

The exercise written below has 4 beats or claps. On claps 1 and 3 say the word “chicken’s” and on claps 2 and 4 say “feet”.

This time, use the two syllables of “chicken's” and make the first part of the word quicker than the second. The “-kens” is longer than “chic-” but still in the space of 1 clap.

The rhythm below, a semiquaver to dotted quaver followed by a crotchet, is very common within strathspeys. Repeat this exercise until you are comfortable with the quicker first note and longer second note within one beat.

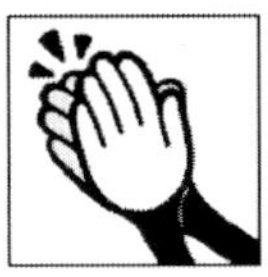

Ex. 2

Track 35

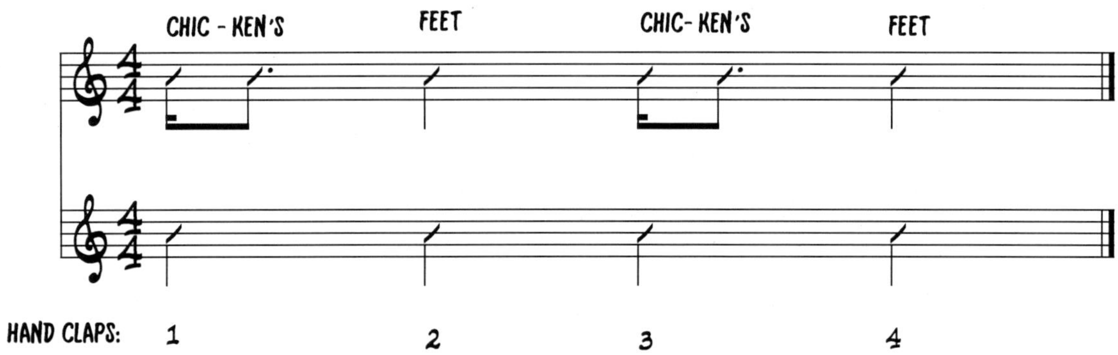

Let's look at how we count the semiquavers and dotted quavers.

For a grouping of semiquavers you count “1-it-is-a” in the space of one crotchet beat.

In beat 2, you can see a semiquaver followed by a dotted quaver. Count the semiquaver as ”2”, then the dotted quaver as “it-is-a”.

Beat 3 is a reversal of beat 2, so for the dotted quaver count “3-it-is” and for the semiquaver count “a”.

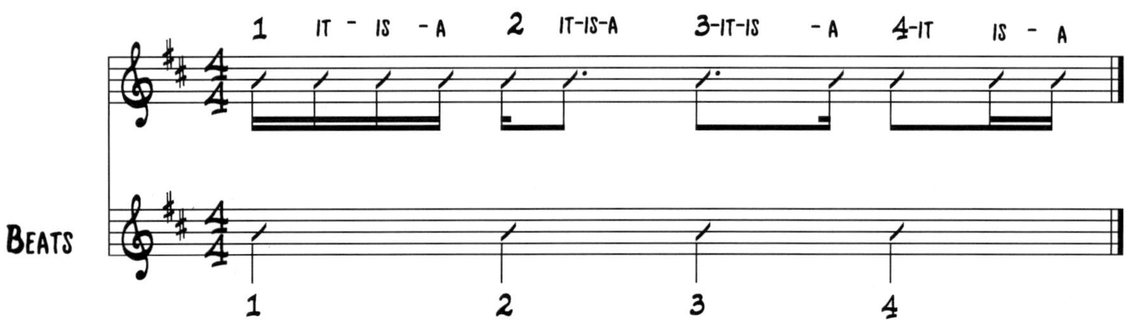

Ex. 3
Track 36

In the clapping exercise below, you are going to say "1-it-is-a", "2-it-is-a", and clap as you say it.

This is how you should count the semiquaver to dotted quaver, on beats 1 and 2. On beats 3 and 4, it reverses and you will learn how to count the dotted quaver to semiquaver.

This is a good place to start learning strathspey rhythms.

Begin the exercise slowly and build up speed. Master these rhythms before moving on.

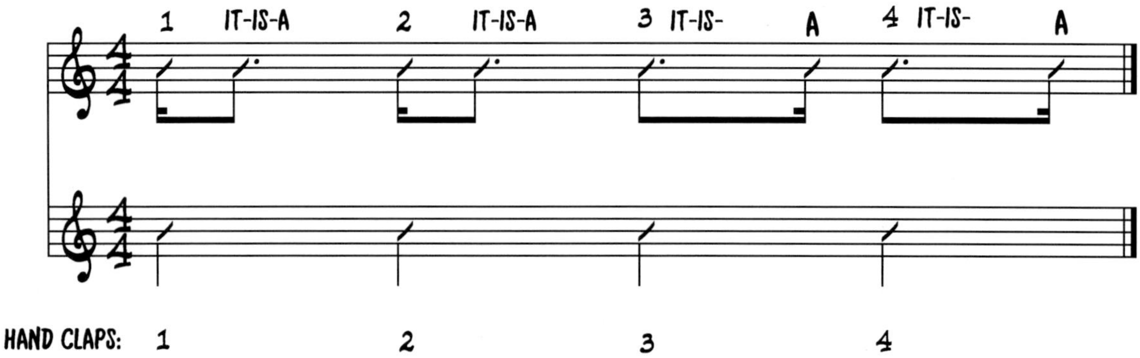

Time to play your first Strathspey!

Ex. 4
Track 37

The tune below contains rhythms you have already learned.

Within the first bar you will see the "chicken's feet" rhythm. Watch out for bar 2 as it changes.

Learn the tune slowly and keep the right hand smooth (legato).

Even with the semiquaver to dotted quaver rhythm at the start of the 1st bar, keep it smooth. Think of passing one note to the next without a gap.

When you can play the melody, move on to playing both hands together.

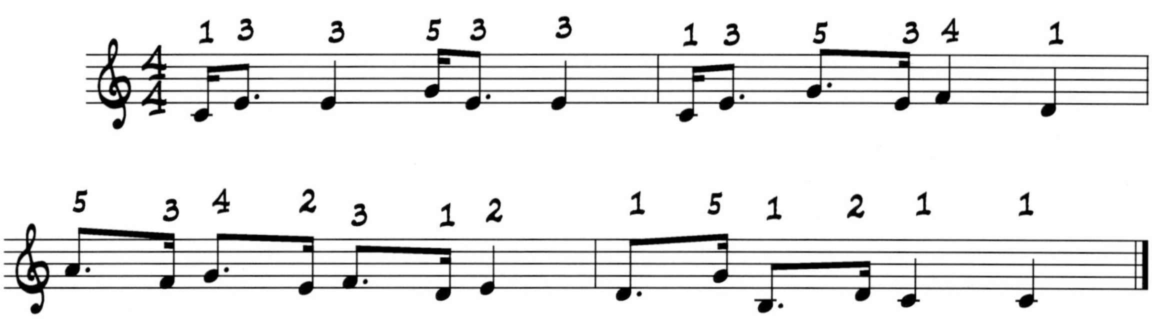

How to play both hands at once

Before we add both hands together, you need to learn the left hand for the strathspey melody from Ex. 4. Learn the melody well, as your right hand will soon be busy too!

Just as in the previous left-hand exercise (Ex. 1 on p. 41) you will find alternating bass notes and chords then both together.

For on the left hand in the first line, you remain on C bass and the C major chord. Remember to maintain your triangle!

The second line requires the bass and chord together.

Ex. 5

Track 38

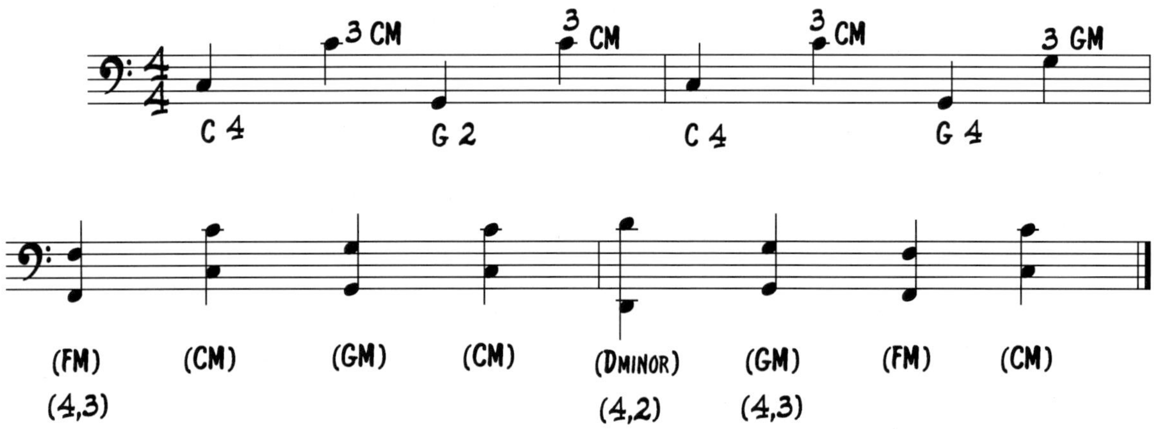

Now it's time for both hands at once!

From the previous exercises you should have a good understanding of what to do.

Remember – go slowly and learn one bar at a time. Focus on playing the melody legato without any gaps, and keep the left-hand notes crisp and short (staccato).

Ex. 6

Track 39

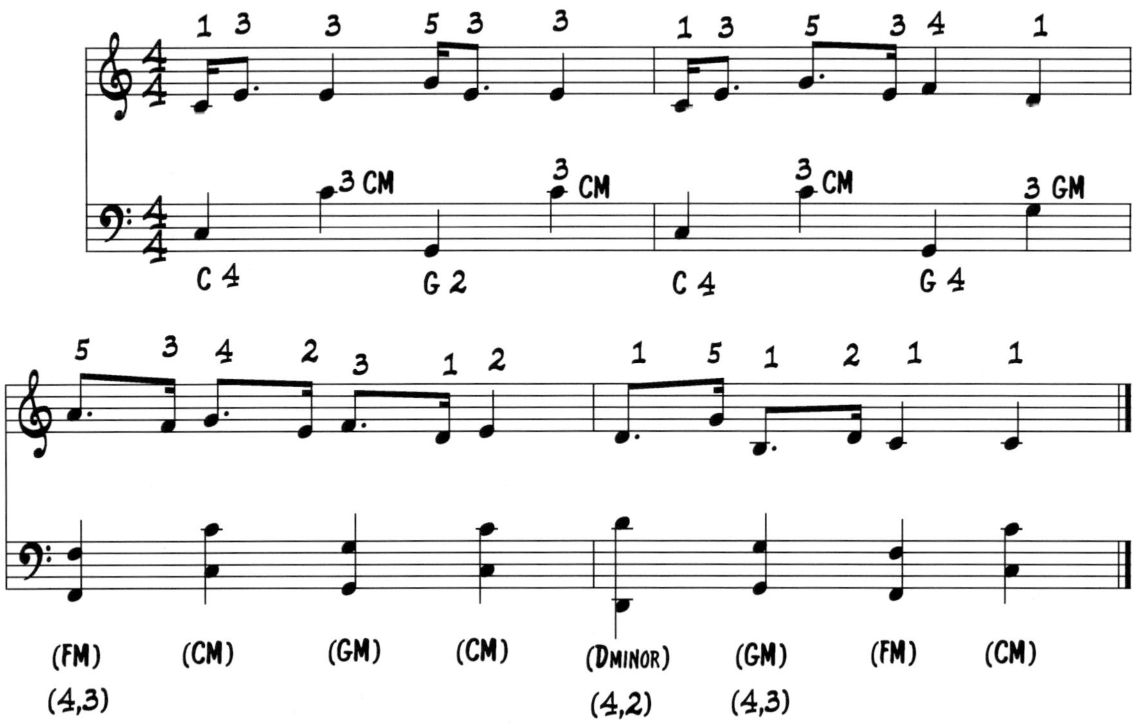

Other Strathspey Rhythms

Other common rhythms you will see in strathspeys are quaver triplets and semiquavers.

Let's start with the quaver triplet as written below. Notice that you have 3 quavers played in the space of 2.

You can count Ex. 7 "one trip-let, two trip-let, three trip-let" "Four."

When played with the bass, the 3 quavers from the triplet fit within 1 bass crotchet.

Start this exercise by clapping the crotchet beat, saying "one trip-let, two trip-let" etc.

When you feel confident with the placement of the quaver triplet, try it with your accordion.

Keep the triplets nice and smooth and go slowly. Make sure the first note of each triplet coincides with the bass and chord.

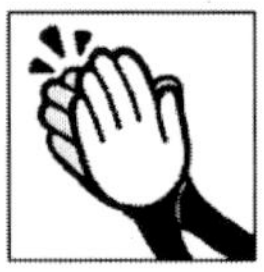

Ex. 7a

Track 40

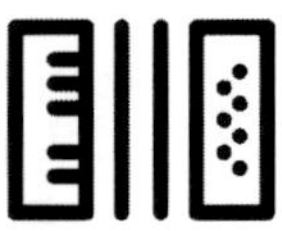

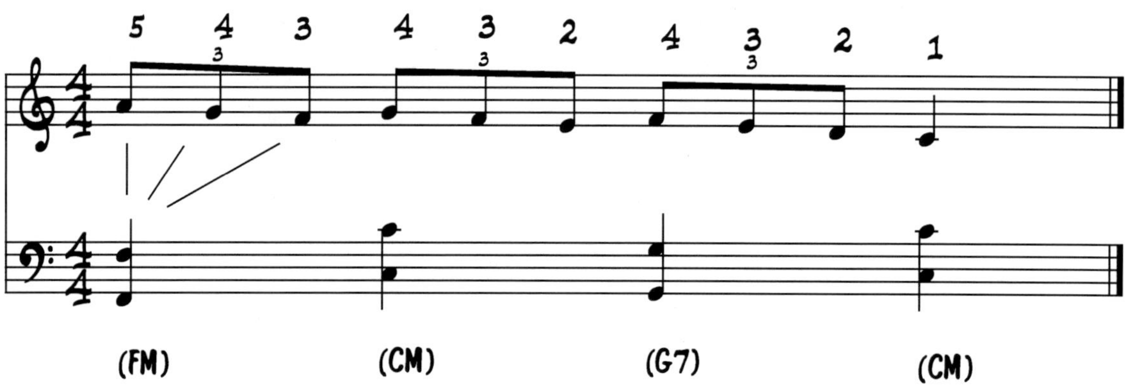

Ex. 7b

Track 41

Semiquaver runs are also very common in strathspeys.

In Ex. 2, you came across semiquavers, but this time you are going to play them with both hands.

Just like the previous exercise, clap the crotchet beats but this time say, "1 it is a", "2 it is a", "3 it is a", "4".

When you feel confident with the semiquaver rhythm, try playing it on your accordion. Again, go slow and keep the semiquavers even. Make sure the first note of each group of four lands at the same time as the bass and chords.

Ex. 8a

Track 42

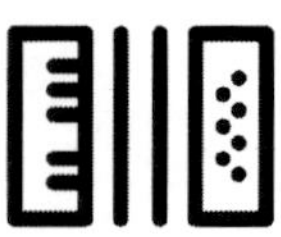

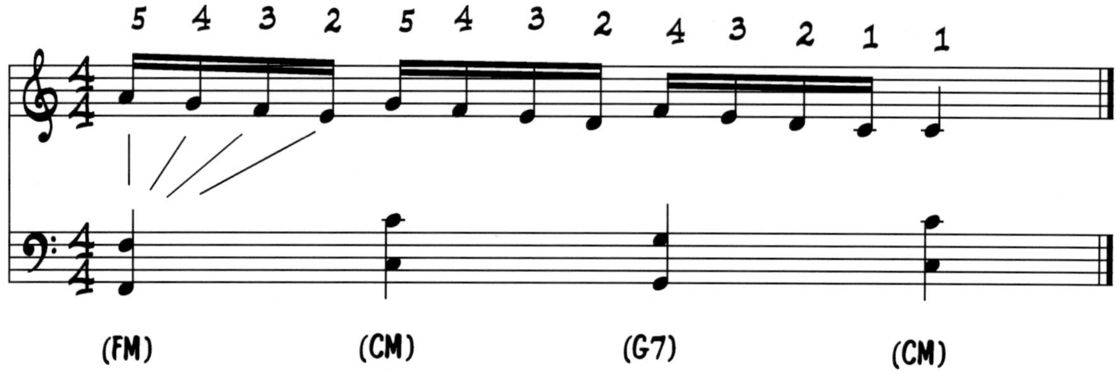

Ex. 8b

Track 43

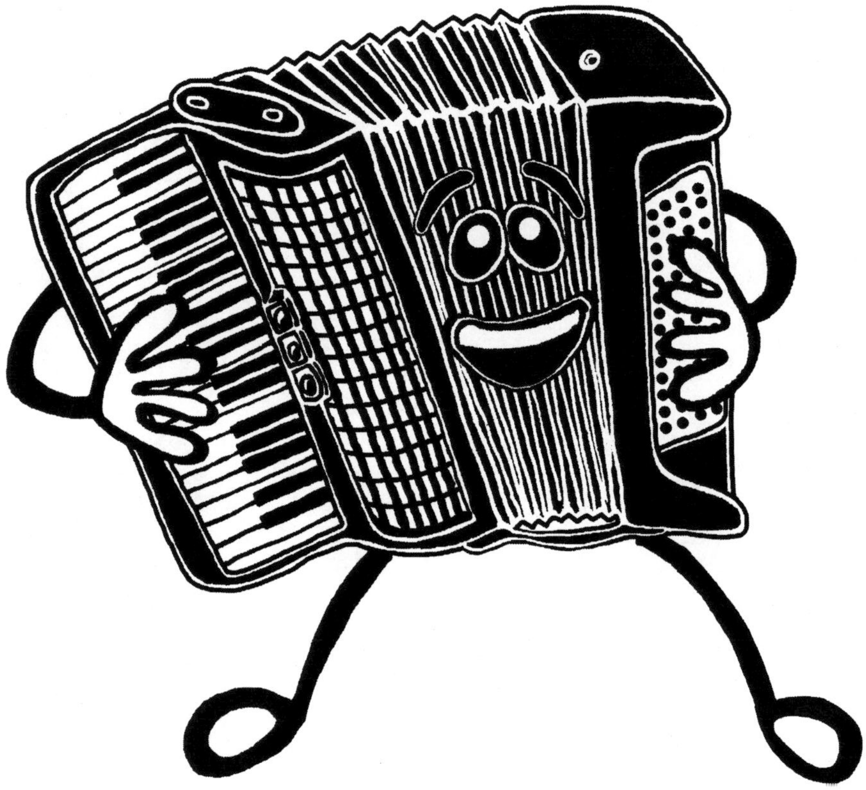

This page has been left blank to
avoid an awkward page turn.

Time to Play

Let's revisit "Lachlan's Bounce" from earlier in the chapter.

Consider all the skills you have learned throughout this chapter and apply them here.

It's time for you to learn the melody. Watch out for now familiar rhythms, use the fingering shown and keep the right hand smooth with no gaps.

Learn the left hand separately. Watch out for the times when you must play bass and chords together, and when the bass moves independently in relation to the chords.

Remember – go slow. Practice one bar at a time, then go back and add two bars together.

Lachlan's Bounce

Ex. 9

Track 44

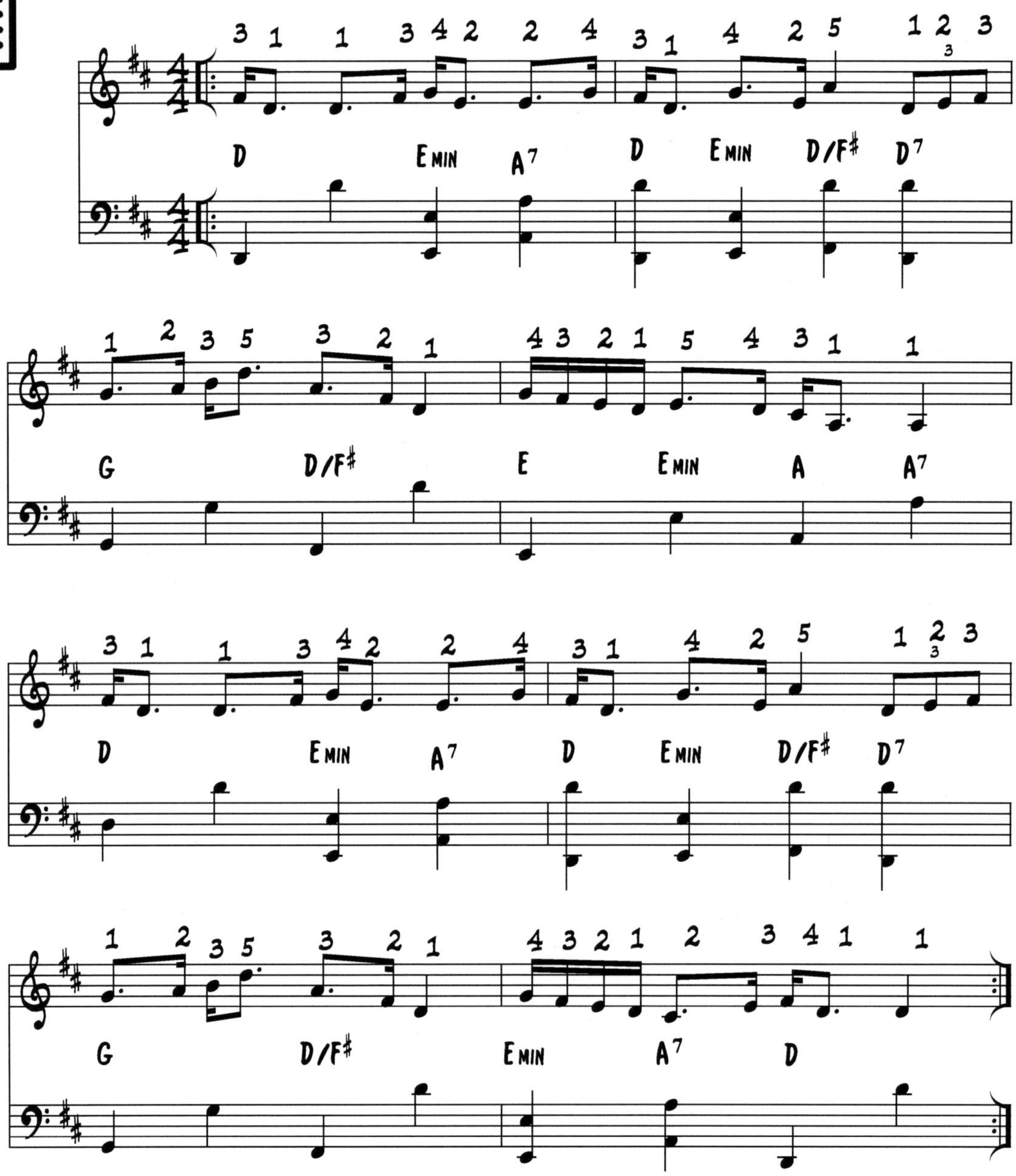

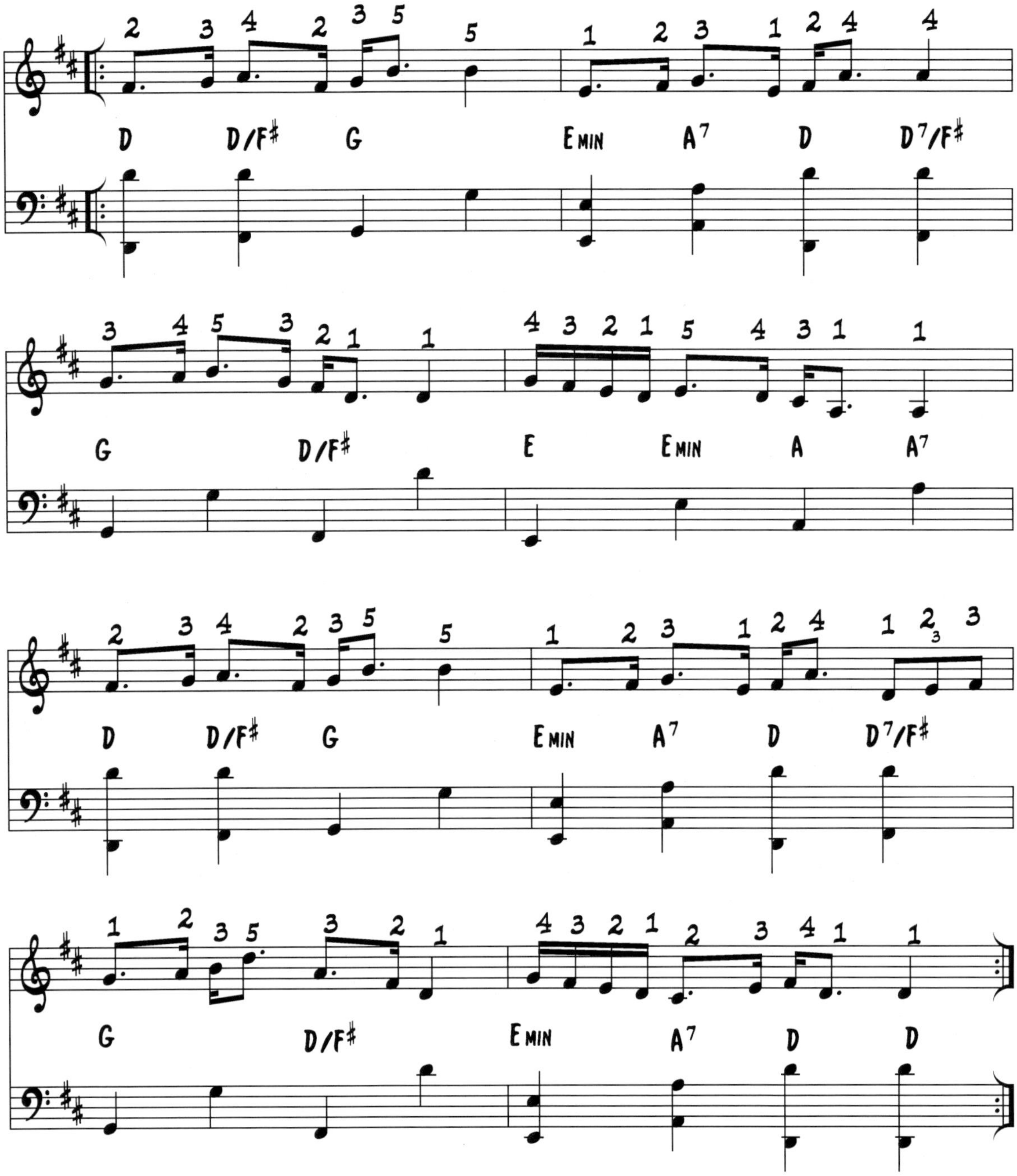

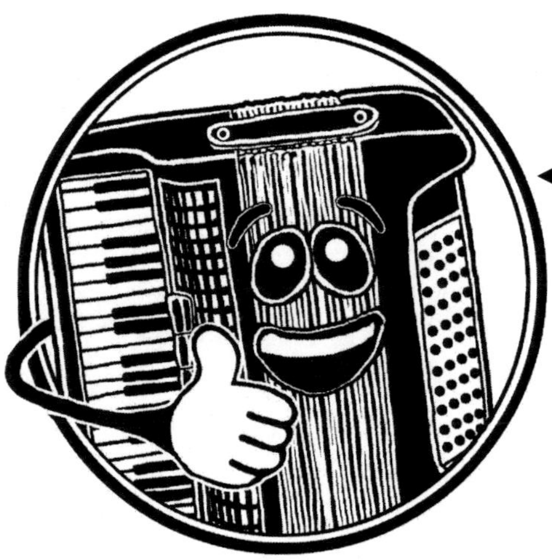

Well done! You have finished the strathspey chapter.

Question - What highland dance would require you play a strathspey?

Answer - The Highland Fling

Grace Notes
"Acciaccatura"

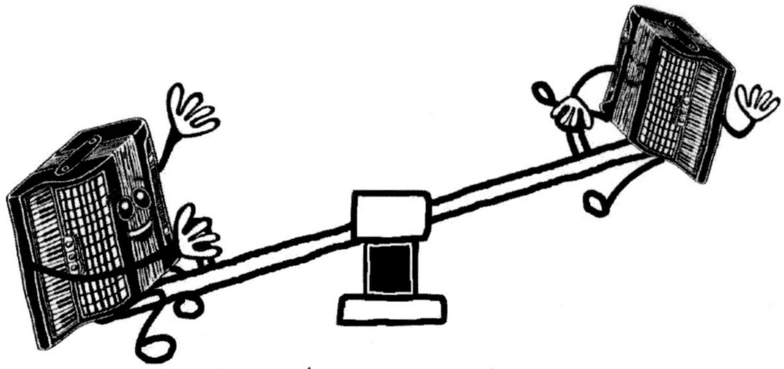

The heavier note stays down

What are grace notes?

Grace notes are little notes added as ornaments to give a graceful effect. They have no time value and should be played as quickly as possible. It is very common in traditional accordion music to play grace notes simultaneously with the main note. The effect is a pleasing sound when the main and grace notes become crushed together.

Why do we use grace notes?

Grace notes originate from the bagpipes. The volume of the bagpipes is steady and the instrument plays constantly, therefore the dynamics can't change. Grace notes are added to the melody to emphasize certain notes. They are also used to distinguish a single note played two or three times in a row.

The accordion doesn't have this dynamic restriction, but grace notes are still used to give a flavour of the bagpipe origins.

Bagpipers have many different rudiments they use to create interest within the melody. When playing the accordion we tend to use grace notes that crush into the main melody note. This can help define the Scottish sound you are trying to create.

It is important that you use grace notes sparingly and subtly within your playing. As the chapter goes on, you will learn where and how to use them. They are mostly used in strathspeys and marches where there is time to play them. You can still play them in reels and jigs but the melody tends to be busier with less opportunity to use them wisely.

What do grace notes look like when written?

Generally speaking, you wouldn't see grace notes written in traditional music for the accordion, unless the composer wanted you to play *exactly* what they intended.

As a performer, you can add grace notes to the piece. Within this chapter you will learn how, where and when to add them in a pleasing way.

Below are two examples of how grace notes can appear in Scottish music. Sometimes a little slur line is indicated, coming from the grace note to the main note. You will see this in the first example.

The second example is from "Lachlan's Bounce," the strathspey you learned earlier.

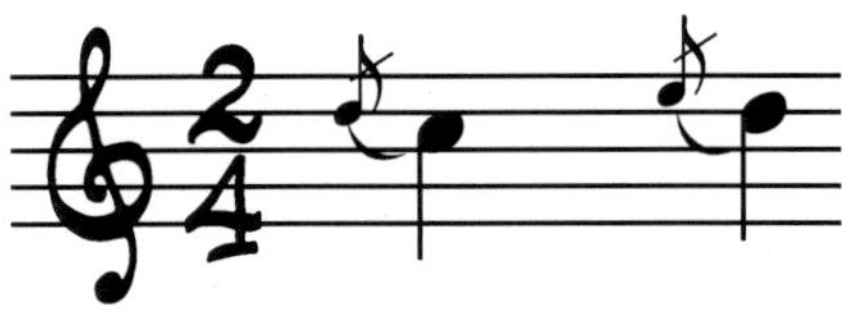

Grace note example 1

In the first example you will see the grace notes are written as a quaver with a diagonal line going through the stem and flag. While grace notes have no rhythmic value, the pitch is as written.

Grace notes are most often pitched a semitone above or below the main note, but can also be a tone, a forth, a fifth or even as octave away. Keep a close eye on the sheet music to play marked intervals correctly, and think smart when adding your own grace notes.

Lachlan's Bounce

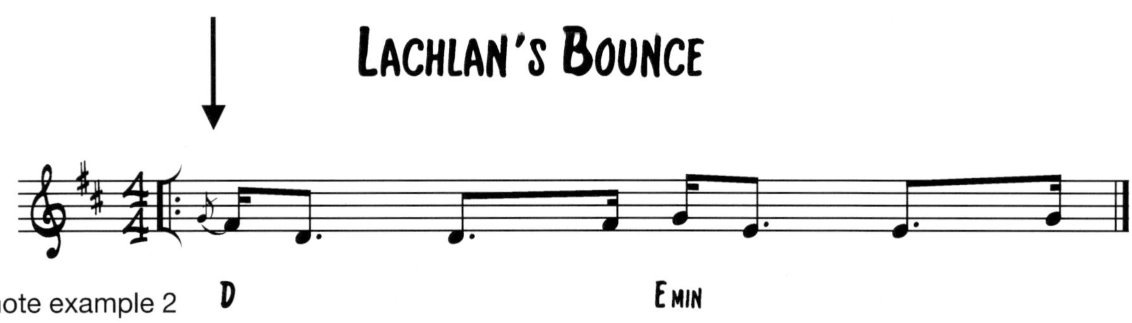

Grace note example 2

How do you play grace notes?

In the first exercise you are going to emulate the sound of the bagpipes when practicing your first grace notes.

Look at the exercise below. Play the two notes, C and G (an interval of a perfect 5th), with your 1st and 4th finger.

Continue to hold them down and with your 3rd finger, lightly and quickly play the F♯. Think about almost flicking the F♯.

By doing this, you are creating the bagpipe's drone sound and adding a grace note all in one little practice exercise.

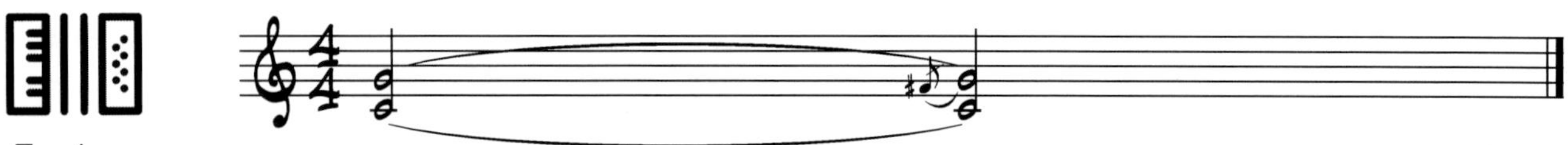

Ex. 1

Track 45

Let's look at how you would play a grace note within a tune.

As previously mentioned, think about *crushing* the notes together. The main focus is on the main melody note and that is where the weight of your finger should go.

Let's do this exercise below. Look at the image of the two characters on the seesaw. Imagine both jump on it exactly at the same time. The heavier one will be the one that stays down and the lighter will go up.

Now it's your turn to try with two notes. Imagine the seesaw, both notes go down at the same time but the grace note is released very quickly.

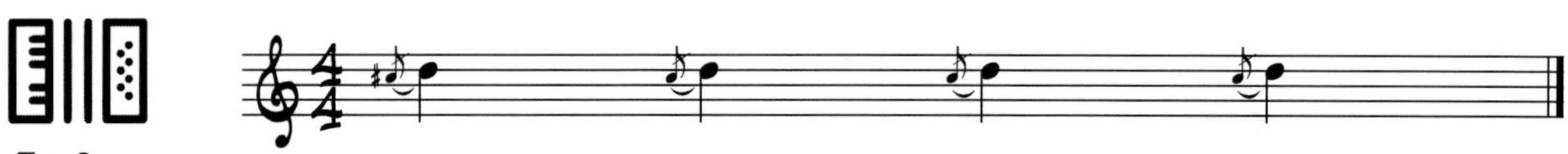

Ex. 2

Track 46

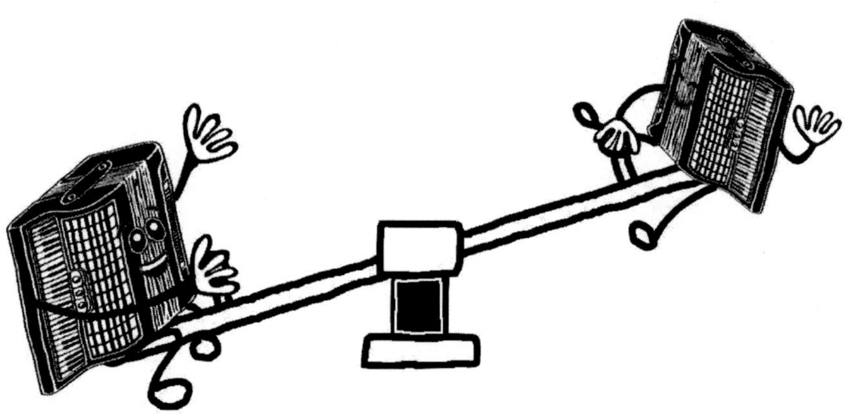

Where are grace notes placed in a tune?

It is up to the performer to decide where grace notes are placed and how they are used.

Let's look at the first two bars of the strathspey "Lachlan's Bounce". The grace notes are written in and the fingering for them is in brackets.

Practice these two bars with the right hand only. Make sure the grace note and main note go down together, but release the grace note quickly.

Lachlan's Bounce

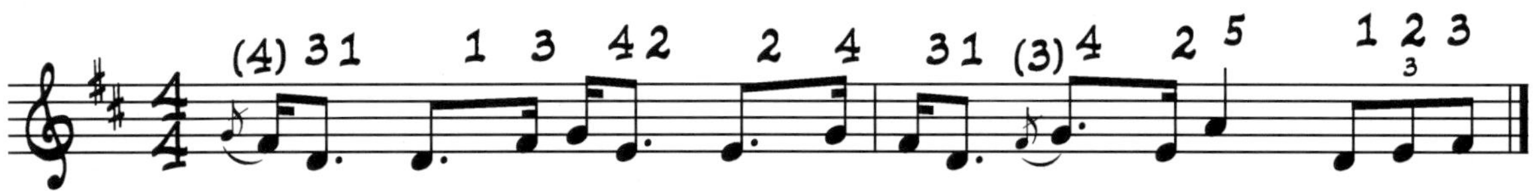

Ex. 3

Track 47

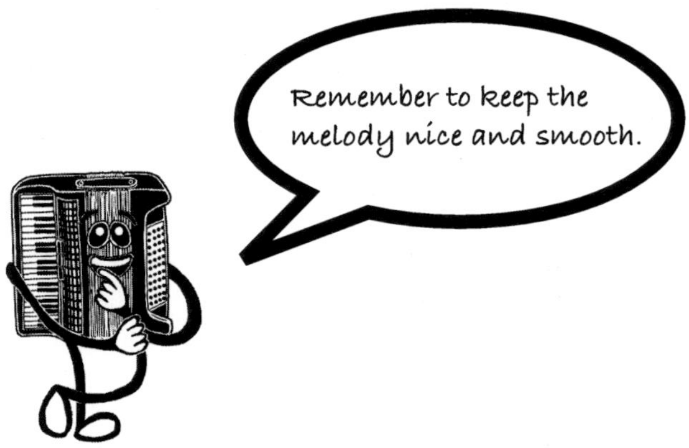

Now you have a better understanding of how to play grace notes, let's do the same two bars again, both hands together.

Make sure you keep the grace note in sync with the main note and avoid playing it early. Really focus on both hands together and go slow. Remember to play the grace note quickly and keep the melody nice and smooth.

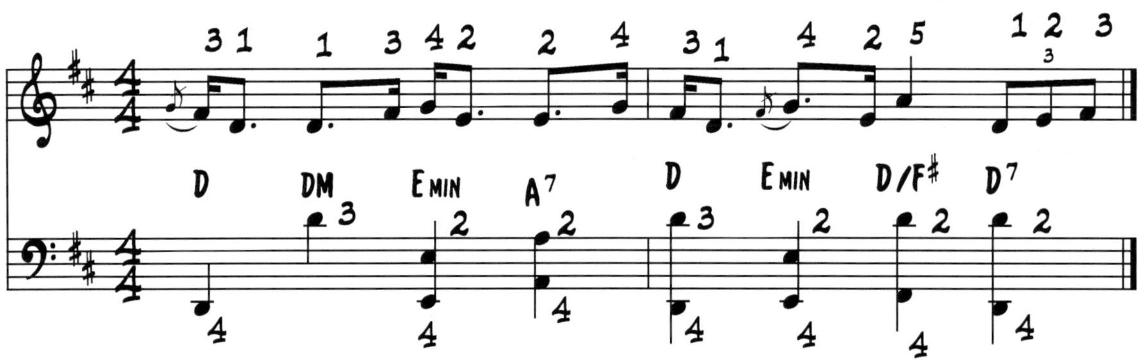

Ex. 4

Track 48

Here is the full strathspey with all the grace notes marked in.

Practice it slowly and pay close attention to the grace notes and the fingering for them too.

Lachlan's Bounce

Ex. 5
Track 49

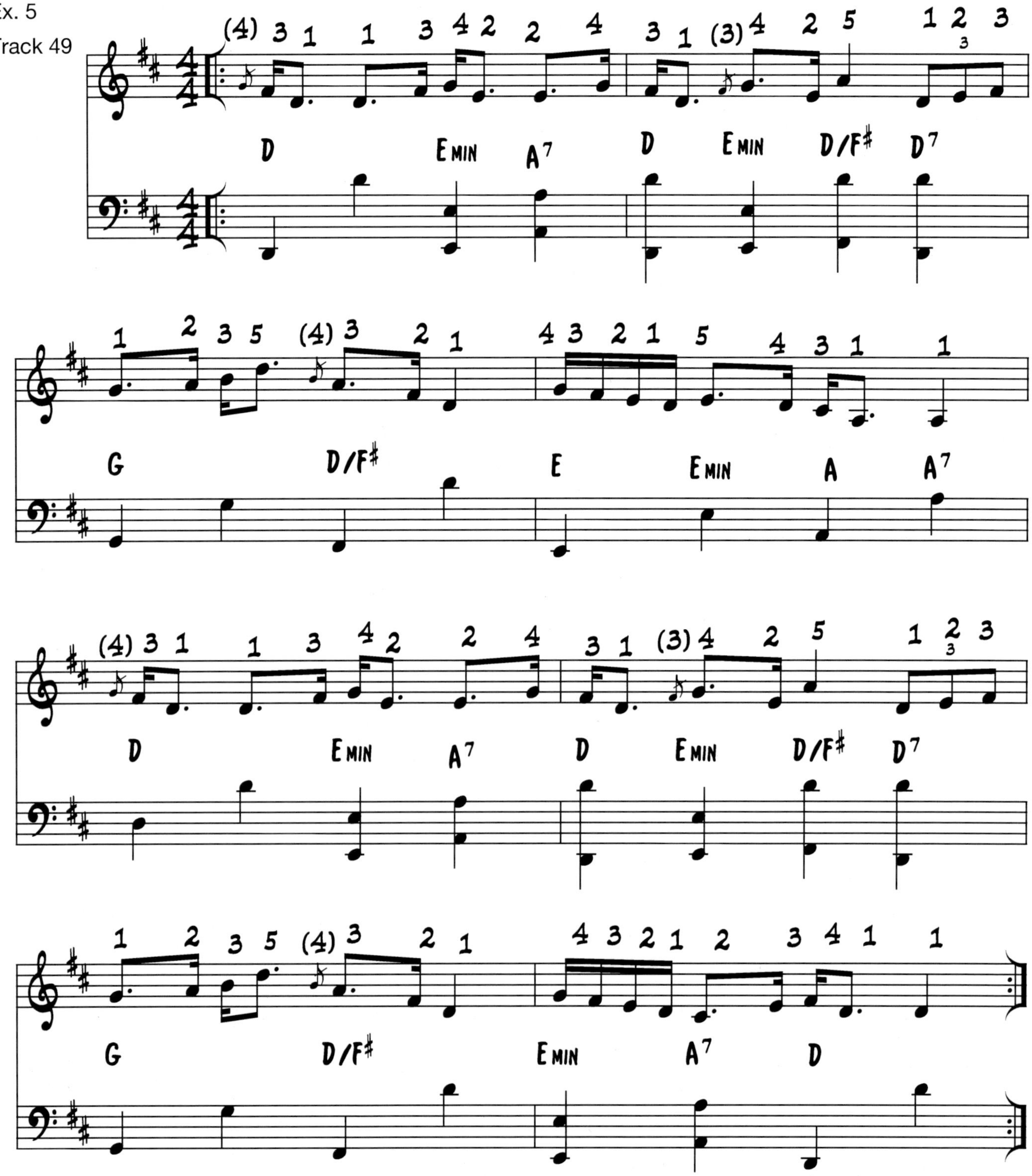

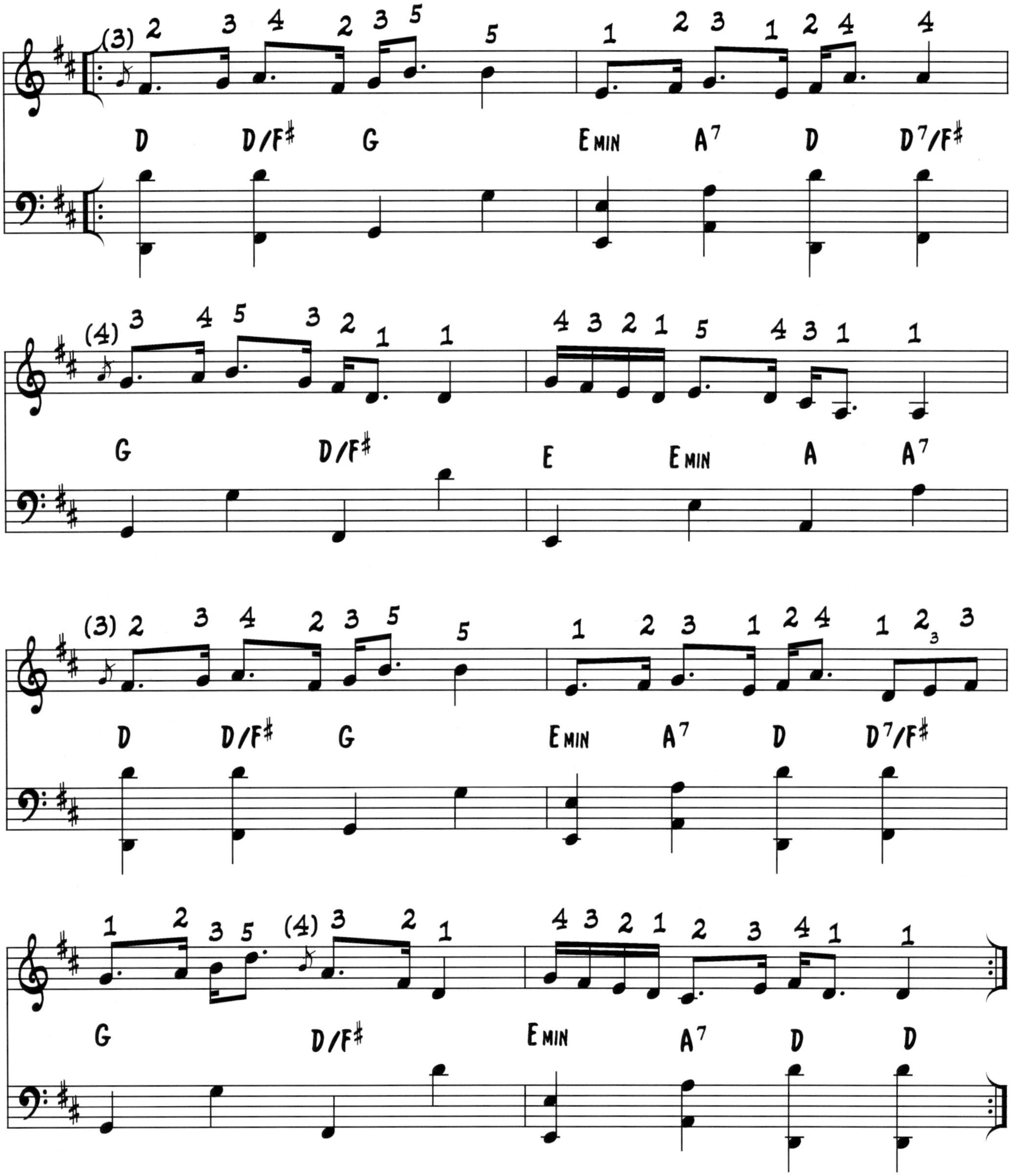

Well done! You have completed the “Grace Notes” chapter.

Accents, Bellows and Phrasing

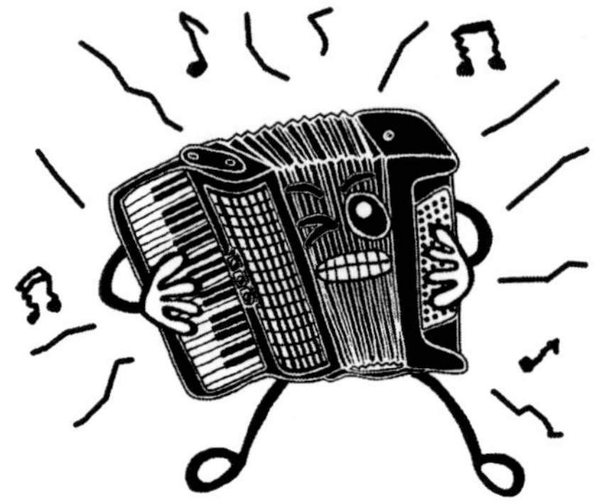

What is an Accent?

An accent is used to highlight a certain note within a phrase. Rather than playing all the notes at the same volume, accents help you bring a piece of music to life with dynamic color.

Imagine reciting a poem and keeping the same monotone voice all the way through with no expression; it would sound dull and boring. It is exactly the same with traditional music and your accordion playing. You have to find points in the piece to accent so they stand out.

What would it look like?

In the reel below, "The Morning Loop", you will see the little arrowhead beneath the first note.

This is a typical example of how an accent would look.

As previously mentioned, you won't find accents written in traditional tunes, but you will learn where to put them and how to play them.

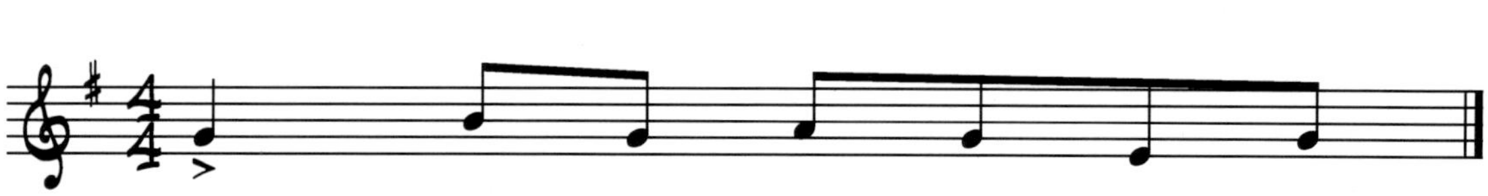

Practice Tip!

When learning pieces, always have a pencil with you and mark in your score where the accents would go. More practice tips in the practice chapter.

How To Play An Accent

To execute an accent, you have to be in control of your bellows.

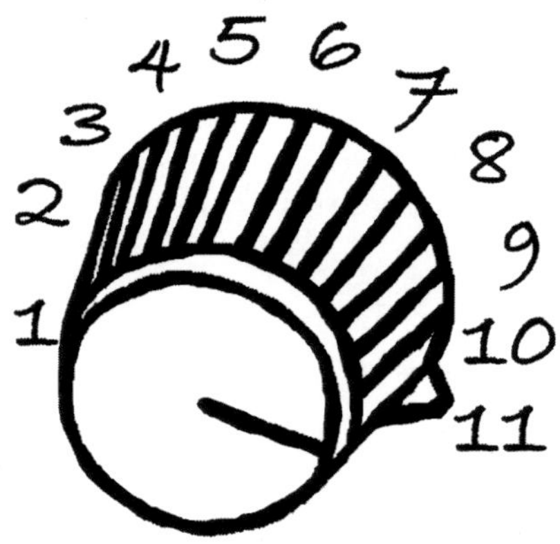

Look at the volume dial opposite. If you are playing a piece at volume 3, an accent needs to quickly head up to 6 then back to 3 on the note. It is a very quick process.

You do this by pulling or pushing the bellows with a short, sharp movement on the note you want to accent.

Imagine you have music playing and your fingers are on the volume dial; you whizz the dial from level 3 to 6 and back again to 3 as quick as you can. This is how a bellows accent should sound.

Let's do the exercise below.

Play middle C for 4 slow beats. On beat 3, place the accent then return to beat 4 at your normal playing level.

Gently guide the bellows out smoothly with even pressure then give a short sharp pull on beat 3. You should hear the volume increase suddenly, then return immediately to your starting volume.

Keep the right hand very smooth and the left-hand notes nice and short. Concentrate on your accents and make sure you can hear and feel the change in dynamics.

The right hand is played in a legato style and you will hear the accent being applied there, the left hand is played in a staccato style and you will hear a slight accent on the bass note.

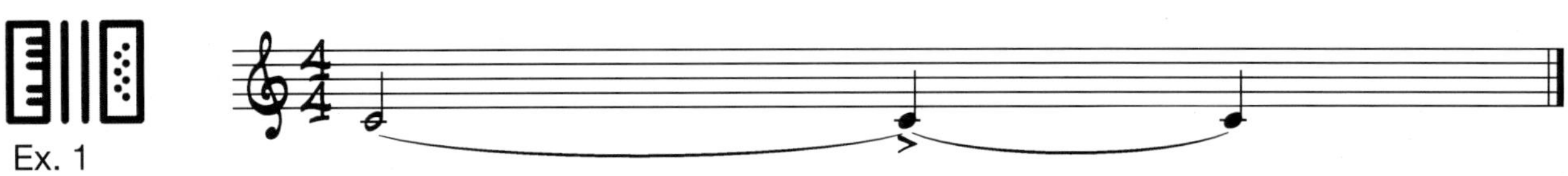

Ex. 1

Track 50

Repeat the above exercise several times until you feel confident with the placement of the accent.

Try this with the bellows going in as well as out. It is important that you are comfortable going either way with the accents.

The next exercise uses both hands together. The accent falls on beats 1 and 3 of the first bar, then on beat 1 of the second bar.

Start with the right hand, and go slowly. Place the accents in the correct position, then move on to playing with both hands together.

Keep the right hand very smooth, and the left-hand notes nice and short. Concentrate on your accents and make sure you can hear and feel the change in dynamics.

Ex. 2

Track 51

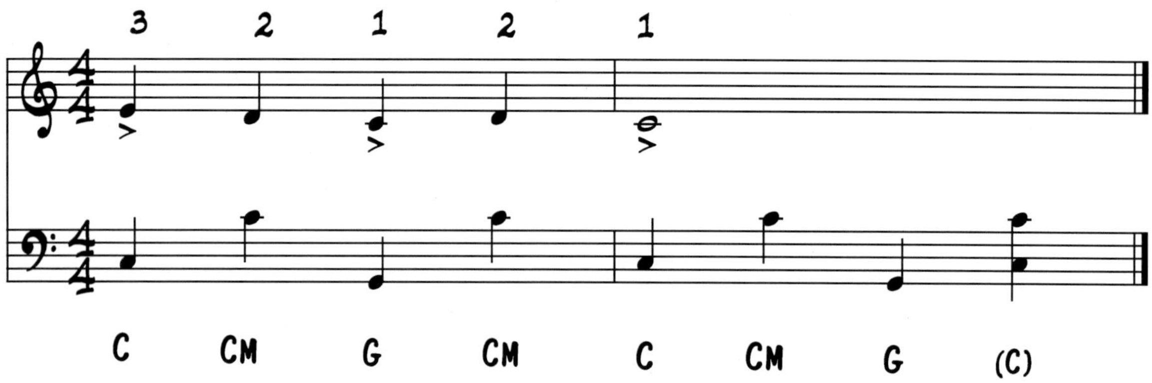

Ex. 3

Track 52

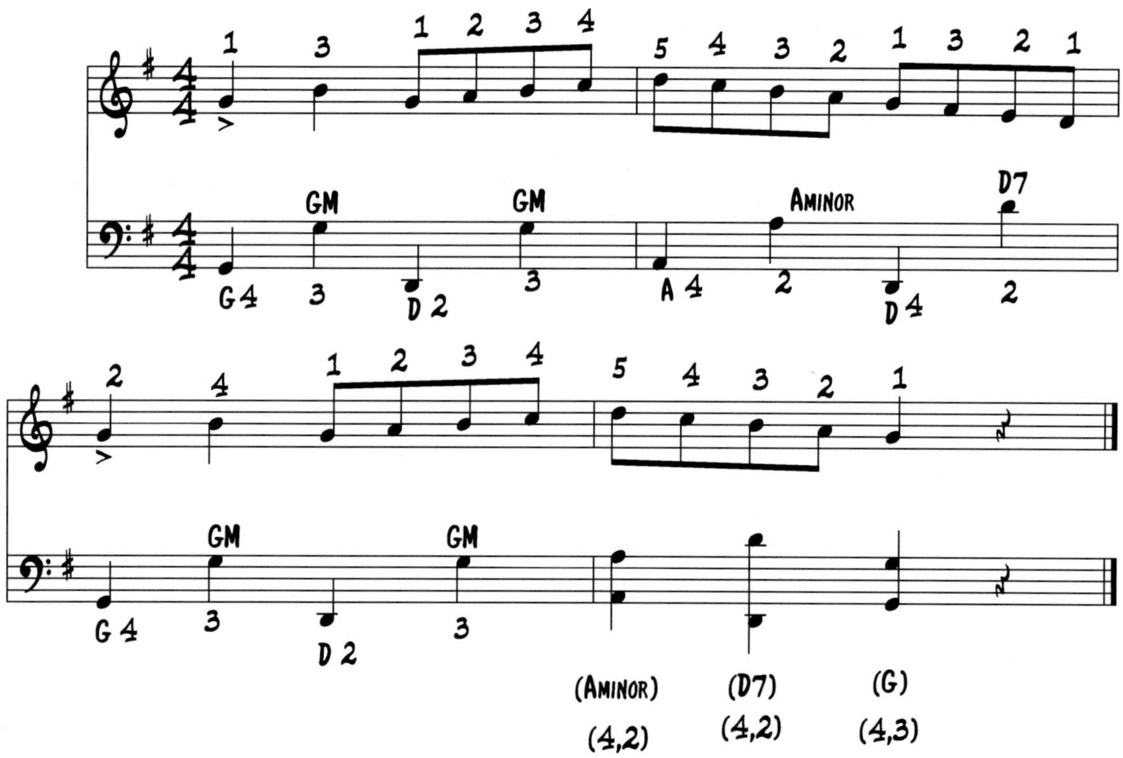

A Little Word About the Bellows

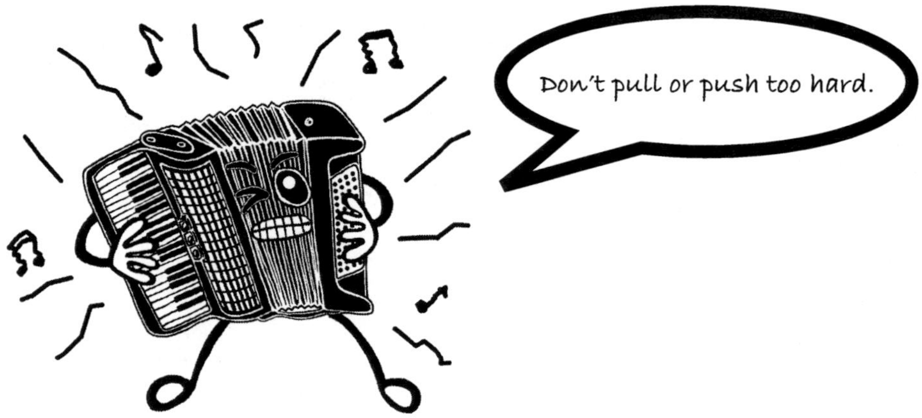

The Bellows

Your use of the bellows brings so much to your accordion playing and it's important you know how to control your bellows correctly.

It is very common for students to pull and push the bellows really hard; this causes your volume to be excessive and not pleasant to the listener. If you are pulling and pushing too hard and always playing at a high volume, it leaves nowhere to go for expression and accents.

Ex. 4

Track 53

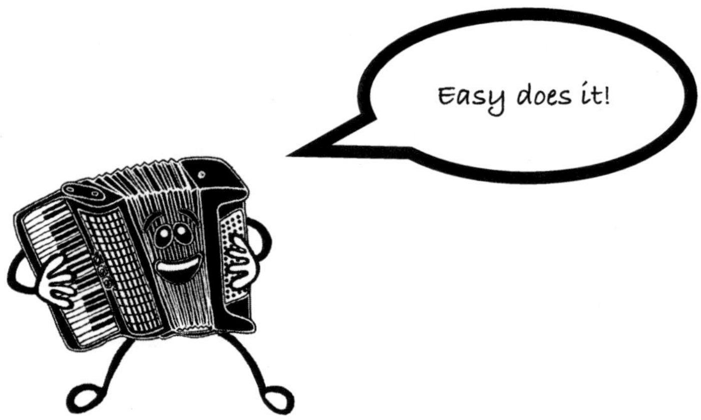

Do this little experiment. Sit with your accordion and play middle C. Remove your left hand from the bellows, but continue to play the right hand. Raise your left hand and wave.

What happens?

The bellows continue towards the floor and the note keeps playing. This experiment shows how little effort the bellows need to power one note. Of course, when you use the bass and play more notes you will use more air, but not as much as you might think.

If it sounds loud to you and you feel exhausted from all that pulling and pushing, then you are using too much muscle on your bellows.

When do you change direction with the bellows?

Think of your accordion bellows as its lungs and notice how it breathes. Look at musical phrases of tunes and sing them through – this is a great way to learn where to change your bellows direction.

Avoid changing direction on a tied note or within a phrase. This is the equivalent of taking a breath half way through a sentence. It just sounds strange.

What is Phrasing?

So far, you have learned three different tunes and types of rhythms within them. This chapter will add to your technical skills and also enhance the way you play traditional Scottish tunes.

Let's look at the first part of a previous reel, "The Fourth Rail Bridge".

When you first play the tune, you should accent the first note of the first phrase. [The phrases have been marked with long curved lines.] The second phrase should be played legato as it contains lots of quavers. Keep this part nice and even. In the half-way phrase, bar 5 you could cut the value of the crotchet. In the score, mark it as a dot above the note – that way you know what it is and what to do.

Looking at the previous phrase, you'll see it has lots of quavers. If you play the first note in bar 5 as the written crotchet, it really put the brakes on. Try cutting it short and then place the accent on beat 2; the B note. This gives a nice feel and musical flow. When you repeat the first eight bars, you can play the first bar like bar 5. Cut the first note short and accent the second beat.

To play your phrases smoothly, make good use of your bellow technique. Maintain constant pressure on your bellows and change direction at the end of a phrase. This helps to keep your playing smooth and not make the bellows change really obvious.

In traditional music the volume of your bellows should be consistent. Whichever direction you are using the bellows, the sound should be balanced and even.

The size of your accordion will determine how many phrases you will be able to play in one direction. A larger accordion should be able to play up to bar 5 in "The Forth Rail Bridge" with the bellows going out and then changing direction. On a smaller accordion, you can change after the first phrase as the bellows are smaller. The legato playing of the phrase is still the same regardless of the accordion size.

The Forth Rail Bridge

Will Marshall

Ex. 5

Track 54

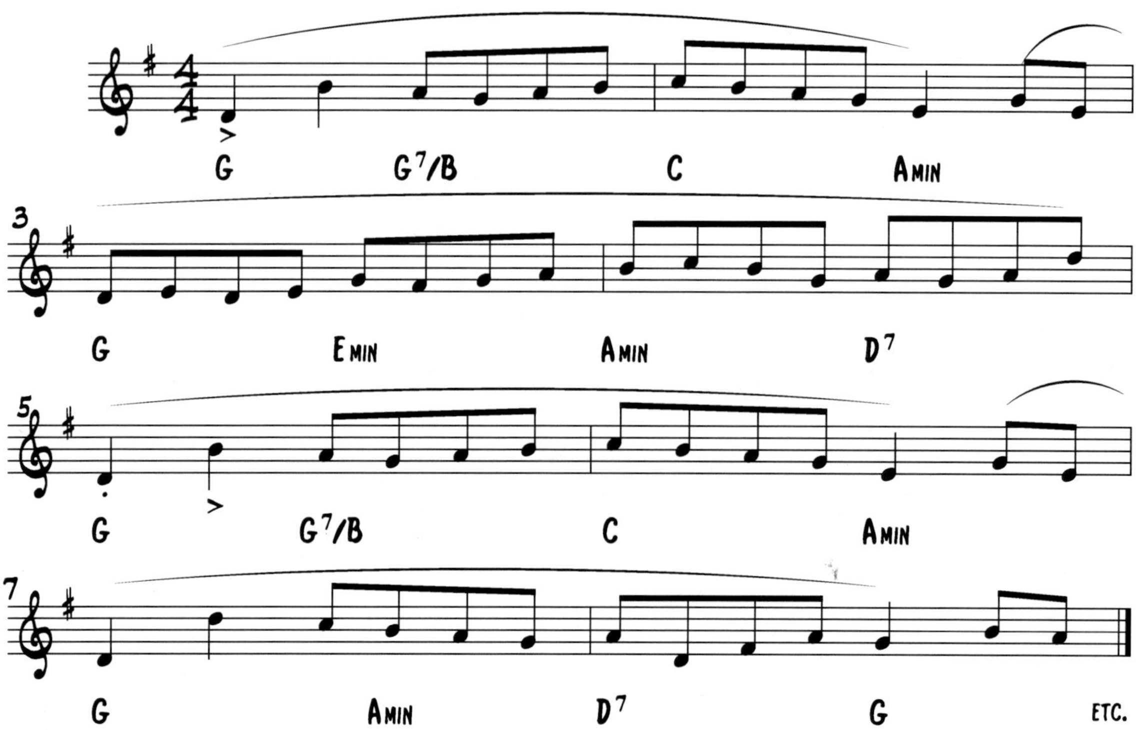

Now, let's look at the 1st part of "Jig for John".

The first accent is on a quaver. Practice this bar with just the right hand and get comfortable with the shorter note while still applying the accent.

Also note the cut note in bar 7. This is to vary the phrasing of the tune. The notes are identical to the bar above and therefore it's a good idea to vary the phrasing of the melody. Cutting the note in bar 7, also provides a nice skip towards the end of the section.

Jig for John

Ex. 6

Track 55

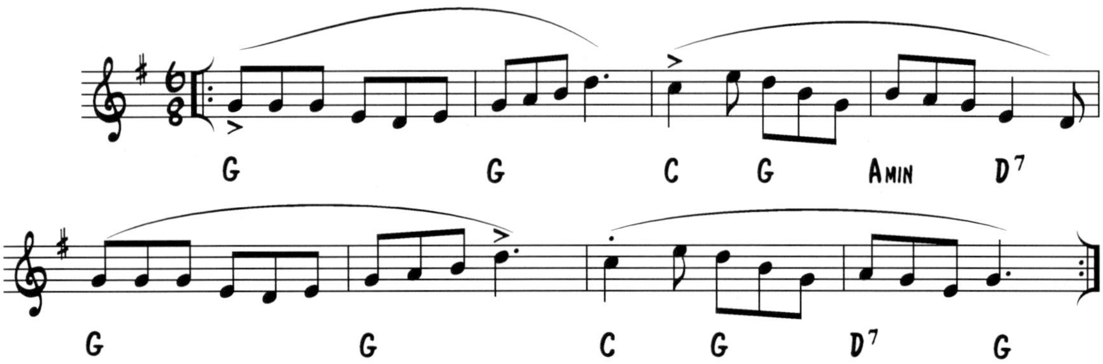

In the strathspey, "Lachlan's Bounce", the first accent is on a semiquaver. It is perfectly fine for the accent to spill over onto the next note.

Notice the cut on the G in the second to last bar. Coming from the triplet before, it's wise to cut the G as it rounds off the triplet run and provides a little space in the melody before the next note.

Lachlan's Bounce

Ex. 7

Track 56

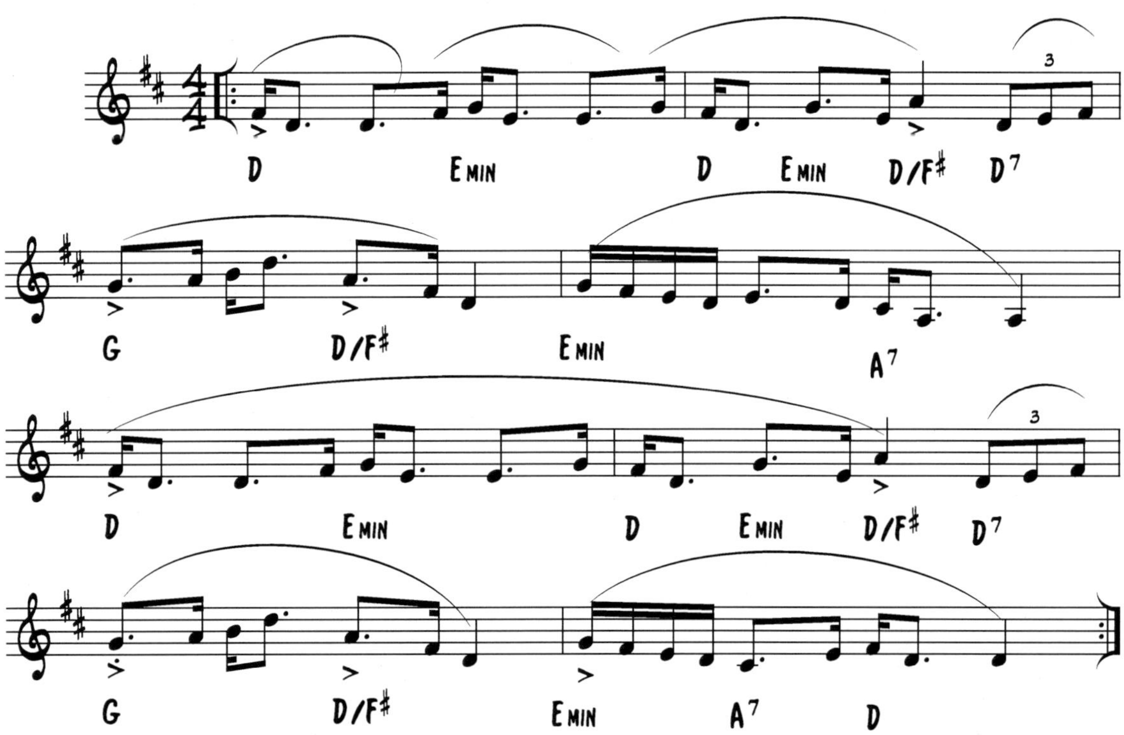

Practice and Mindset

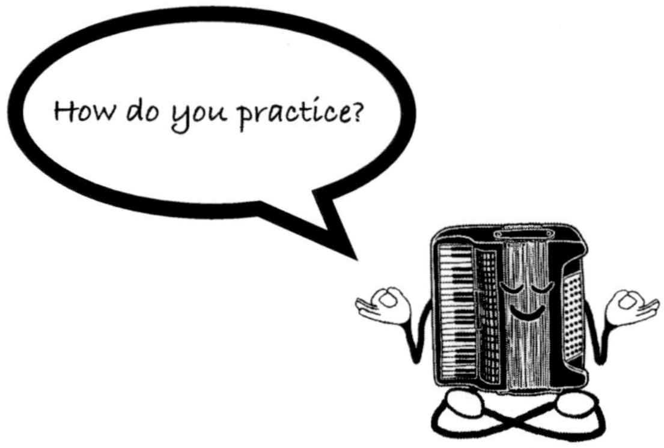

Some tips to help with your practice and mindset

Have you ever heard the phrase "Practice makes perfect?" It doesn't! You can do lots of practicing but you may be repeating the same mistakes every time.

Be efficient in how you practice to get the most out of your sessions.

Your new motto should be "Practice for consistency!"

Before you start your practice, establish goals; not just goals for your practice session that day, but an extended objective too. Plan for a day, a week, a month, three months and a year ahead. Keep a practice diary and make sure it's up-to-date.

I am huge fan of the books *The Art of Being Brilliant* by Dr. Andy Cope, and *Mindset* by Dr. Carol S. Dweck. I highly recommend you read both books, and I shall refer to both in this chapter.

I must thank Dr. Andy Cope as he kindly let me use the "HUGG" diagram in this chapter, which I suggest you fill in. More on this later.

Pre-Practice Routine

Have your practice journal at hand and get yourself ready.

Make sure you have a good chair that allows you to have good posture.

Things to have on hand during your practice sessions.

Music Stand- Make sure you can see your music well.

Current Music to Learn- Keep it on your music stand so you're not searching for it.

Metronome- I recommend a digital model which you can download to your smart phone.

Pencil and Eraser- For marking up your score and taking notes. Don't use a pen!

Your Smart Phone- No, not for taking calls or playing games; you can set a practice timer, use your metronome, record either video or audio and listen back.

Practice Routine

Your schedule and how much time you can commit will determine how long you can practice.

Start with a warm up.

Scales and arpeggios are great for this. You can play these in so many different ways and make them musical. Use the right hand, both hands together, contrary motion, legato, staccato, and every variation you can think of. Play the exercises from earlier in this book too. Scales and arpeggios are such a vital ingredient within traditional music, so get super confident with these and rotate them. For example, start on C, then advance around the circle of 5ths: C, G, D, A etc., then C, F, B♭, E♭ etc. Do the same cycle with arpeggios.

Techniques

Perhaps you are working on a specific technique that requires some attention. It might be a technique within a piece you are working on. Isolate this area and concentrate on it. It might require metronome practice with separate hands, then both together.

Pieces

Is there anything you don't understand in the notes, rhythms or any other aspect of the music you are practicing?

Break the pieces down into little blocks and separate everything: fingering, melody notes, bass and chords, and hand coordination. Take one bar at a time. You can always divide that bar up into little sections. Then do the same on bar two, continuing this process for the entire piece. Your practice session might be focused on two or four measures, depending on what you set out to do. Remember to break everything down into manageable pieces, then add them together.

Get the most out of your practice sessions by setting clear goals.

Set aside time to just play. Let it rip and have fun!

That's why we play a musical instrument: to play music.

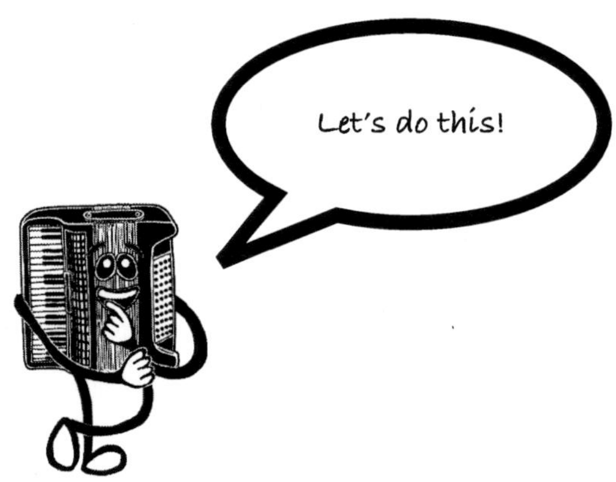

Mindset

Now you know, learning the accordion is hard. You need to accept this then you can get on your journey.

The right mindset is so important in learning and playing music. Dr. Carol Dweck, author of *Mindset*, talks about having either a fixed mindset or a growth mindset.

Fixed Mindset: People with a fixed mindset believe that they are either born good at something or they aren't. This leads them to not work as hard, give up easily and reject constructive criticism.

Example: You have a fixed mindset if after two attempts at playing the accordion you say, "I can't play," and never try again.

Growth Mindset: People with a growth mindset believe that success is a direct result of effort and hard work.

Example: Mozart studied and practiced relentlessly for 10 years before he was able to produce his first successful composition.

Mindset is a learned behavior and can be changed. Moving from a fixed mindset to a growth mindset can feel uncomfortable at first, but with persistence, you can change the way you view your failures and successes. The person who is sure they suck at the accordion, who may feel comfortable at first, will start to improve if they work hard enough and are dedicated to doing so.

Fixed Mindset

"I will look stupid."

"I can't play this."

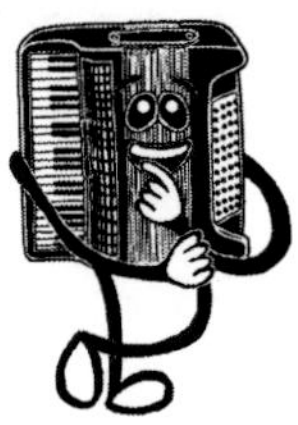

Growth Mindset

"What can I learn?"

"I can't play this, YET!"

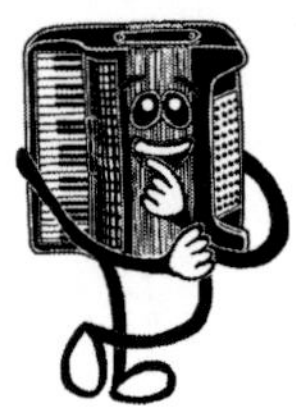

Deliberate Practice

Deliberate practice refers to a special type of practice that is purposeful and systematic. While regular practice might include mindless repetitions; deliberate practice requires focused attention and is conducted with the specific goal of improving performance.

Example: Many great musicians recommend repeating the most challenging sections of a tune until you master them. Virtuoso violinist Nathan Milstein says, "Practice as much as you feel you can accomplish with concentration."

He became concerned because others around him at music school practiced all day long, so he asked his professor how long should he practice. His professor replied, "It doesn't matter how long. If you practice with your fingers, no amount is enough. If you practice with your head, two hours is plenty."

HUGGs

What is a HUGG? It stands for Huge Unbelievable Great Goals. This is the concept of Dr. Andy Cope – author of lots of great books. I derived this section from *The Art of Being Brilliant* where he talks about setting huge goals.

On the next page, Andy has kindly allowed publication of a HUGG diagram where you can fill in your huge goal.

What do you want your huge goal to be? Have a think and write it at the top of the pyramid. It could be performing somewhere, or learning a piece, or recording something, or entering a competition. Think BIG! Really BIG!!!

You can fill-in the rest of the pyramid, including the things you need to do to achieve your goals. Set little goals and complete them.

Think hard about your practice goals and write them into the blocks. Set clear targets.

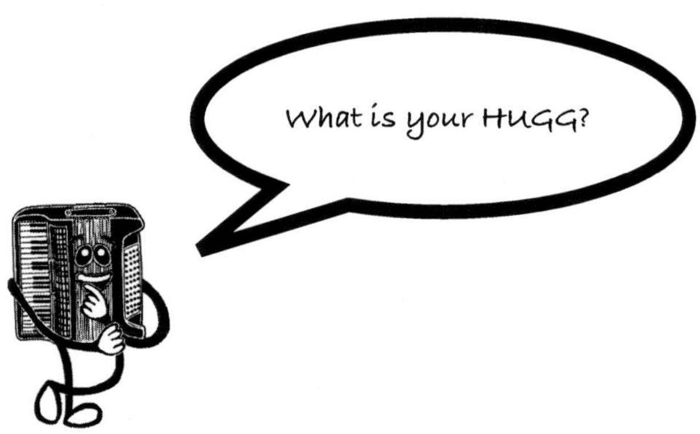

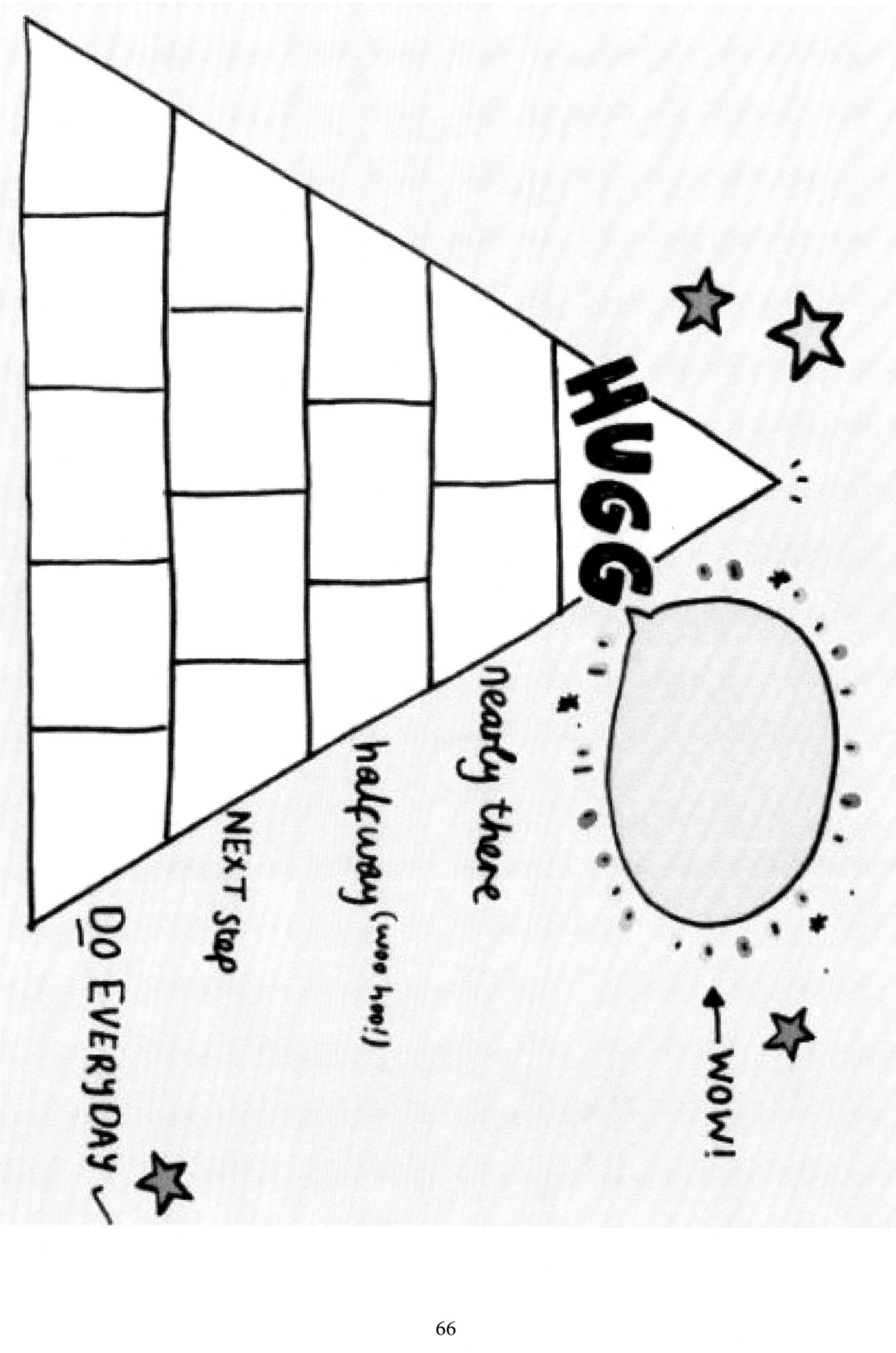
HUGG
← WOW!
nearly there
halfway (woo hoo!)
NEXT step
DO EVERYDAY ✓

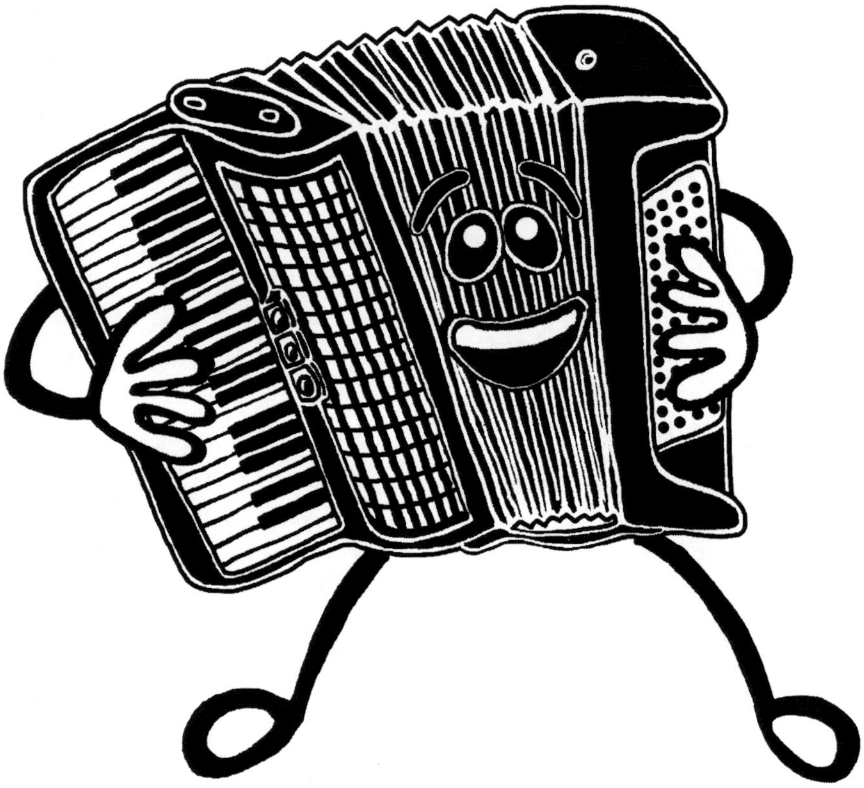

This page has been left blank to
avoid an awkward page turn.

Let's Play!

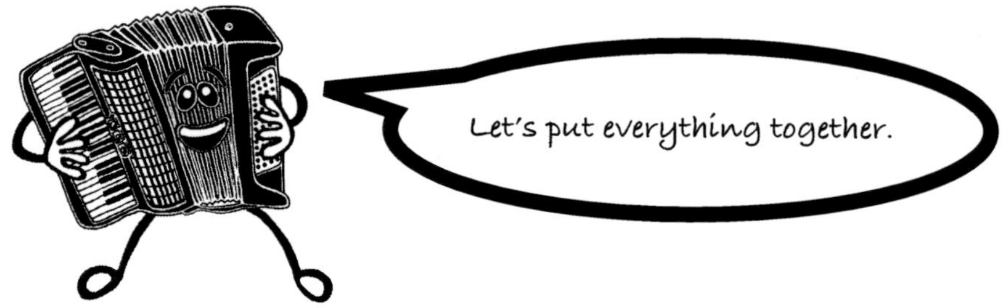

Performances

Now it is time to add all the things you have learned and put them into full tunes. In this chapter, you will play through one strathspey, one jig and two reels.

When playing a reel, jig or strathspey, you can either start with a chord or an introduction.

If you decide to play a chord, this would be the tonic chord of the key of the piece you are playing. Before you play the chord, think of the tune and the speed you would like to play it. Count "1-2" at the speed you want to play, then play the chord.

You could always add an *anacrusis*. This is an upbeat, or pickup note before beat 1 starts.

In the example below you will see where you count the strong beats, the chord and the *anacrusis*. You will notice the *anacrusis* falls on the second part of the bar; if you played it as two quavers in beat 4, it would be too quick.

The G major chord lasts for a whole bar, then emphasized on beat 1 of the following bar with the bellows. With the left hand, play the chord only until the accent, then add the bass note for added punch. At the end of the set, you can also do the same if desired.

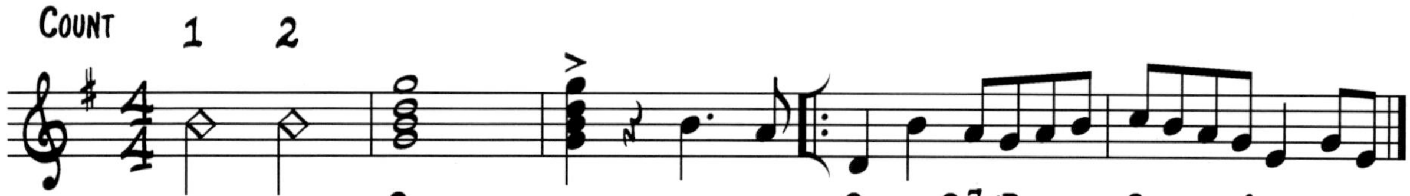

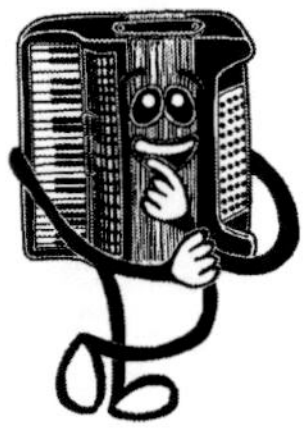

Top Tip!

Remember, counting 1-2 will help dictate the speed you are about to play and cement the 2-in-the-bar feel you are looking for.

You can also play a chord at the end, to indicate that the set of tunes is finished. Chords at the start and end are usually played for the dancers to acknowledge their dancing partner and to signal that the band is starting or finished.

In the example below showing the end of the "Forth Rail Bridge Reel", you will notice that you finish the tune, leaving the first half of the next bar empty then play the chord on the second part of the bar. Hold the chord for the 1-2-1 count and accent the 1 with the bellows.

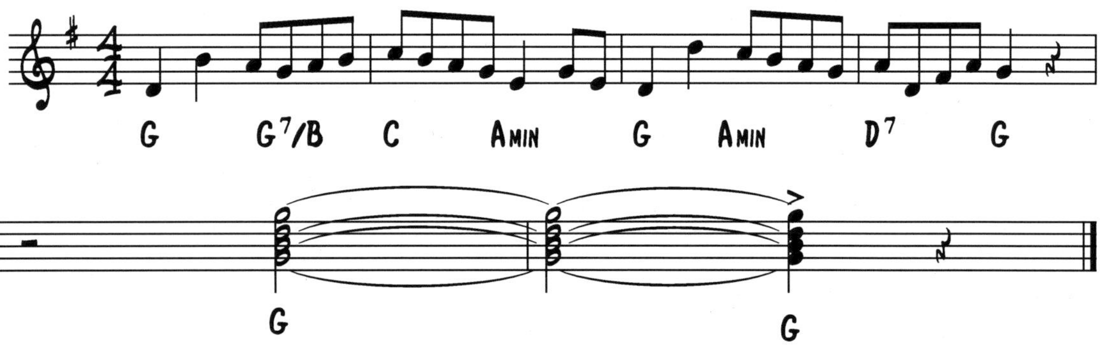

When starting a tune, you could play an introduction instead – perhaps the last 4 bars of the first tune of your medley or set.

Or you can start without a chord or introduction, but it is always a good idea to count 1-2-1.

The *anacrusis* you would play, is on the 2 – the strong beat.

Below is an example of just going straight into the tune by counting the "1-2-1."

The Forth Rail Bridge

Count "1-2-1"

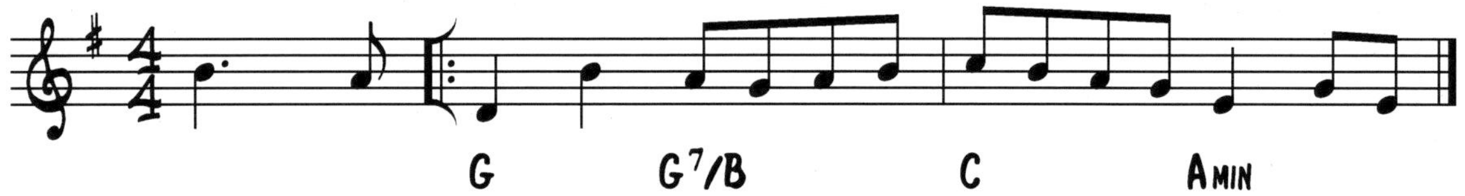

Let's play a Jig!

With "Jig for John," go straight into the tune, but count "1-2-2-2." This will give you a 2-bar count-in at the tempo you want to play the tune. Counting-in is good practice for playing with other musicians.

Ex 1a "Jig for John" lead accordion with band. Ex 1b. Band only

Ex. 1a

Track 57

Ex. 1b

Track 58

Jig for John

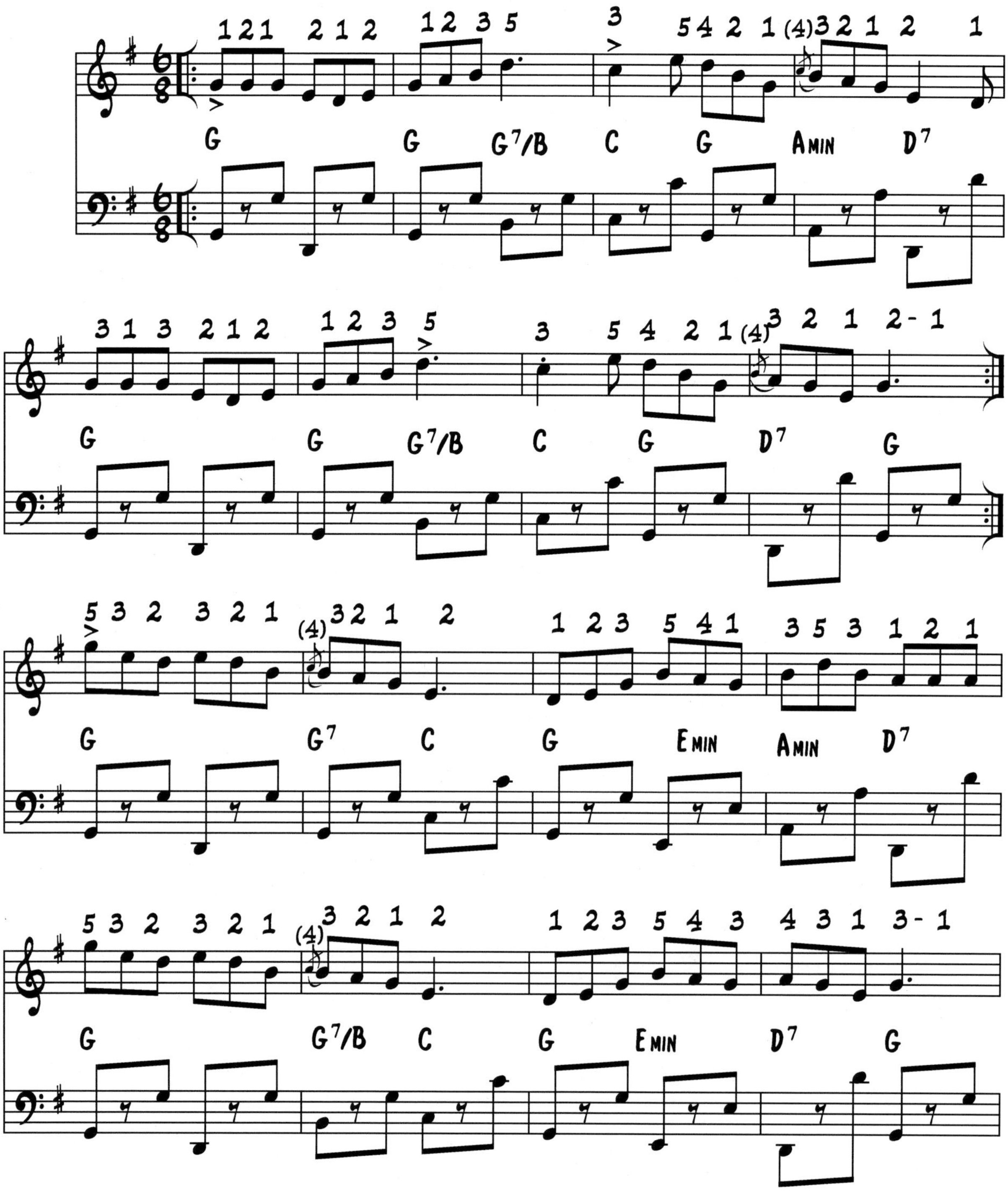

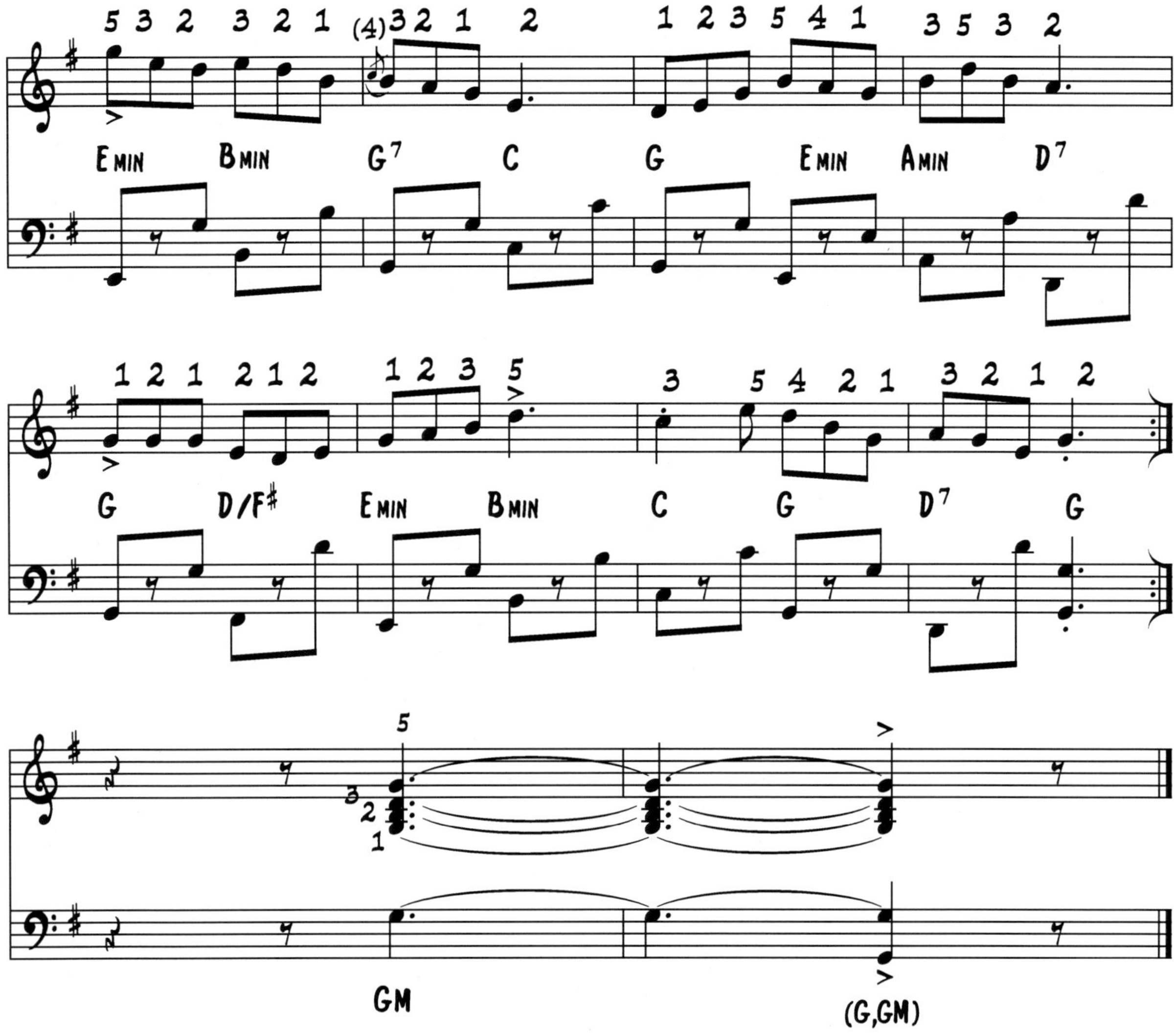

Top Tip

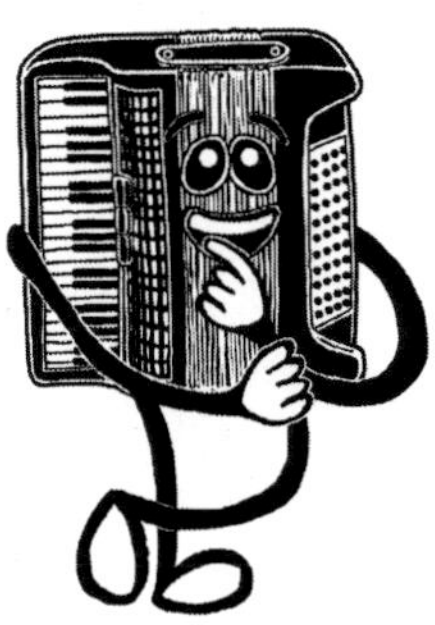

Practice these tunes with a metronome, especially to help with the chords at the beginning and to keep you from speeding up.

If you are playing with other musicians, nod your head to signal when the chord stops. To practice this, count, play the "1-2" chord and nod the finish at the same time. That way everyone will start and finish at the same time.

Let's play Reels!

With this being the last section of the book, you are going to play two tunes in sequence, "The Forth Rail Bridge" and "The Morning Loop".

Count yourself in with "1-2" at the speed you are going to play the reel. Play the introduction chord at this tempo and then go into the reels. Metronome practice is very beneficial for all of these tunes.

Play each tune twice. After the first tune there are two chords, Em and A7, which allow you to move smartly into the new key of D for the second tune. When playing tunes sequentially, think about how you get from one tune to the next smoothly and the style of the tunes. Keep the set of tunes in a similar style.

Ex 2a "Reels" lead accordion with band. Ex 2b. Band only

The Forth Rail Bridge

Ex. 2a
Track 59

Ex. 2b
Track 60

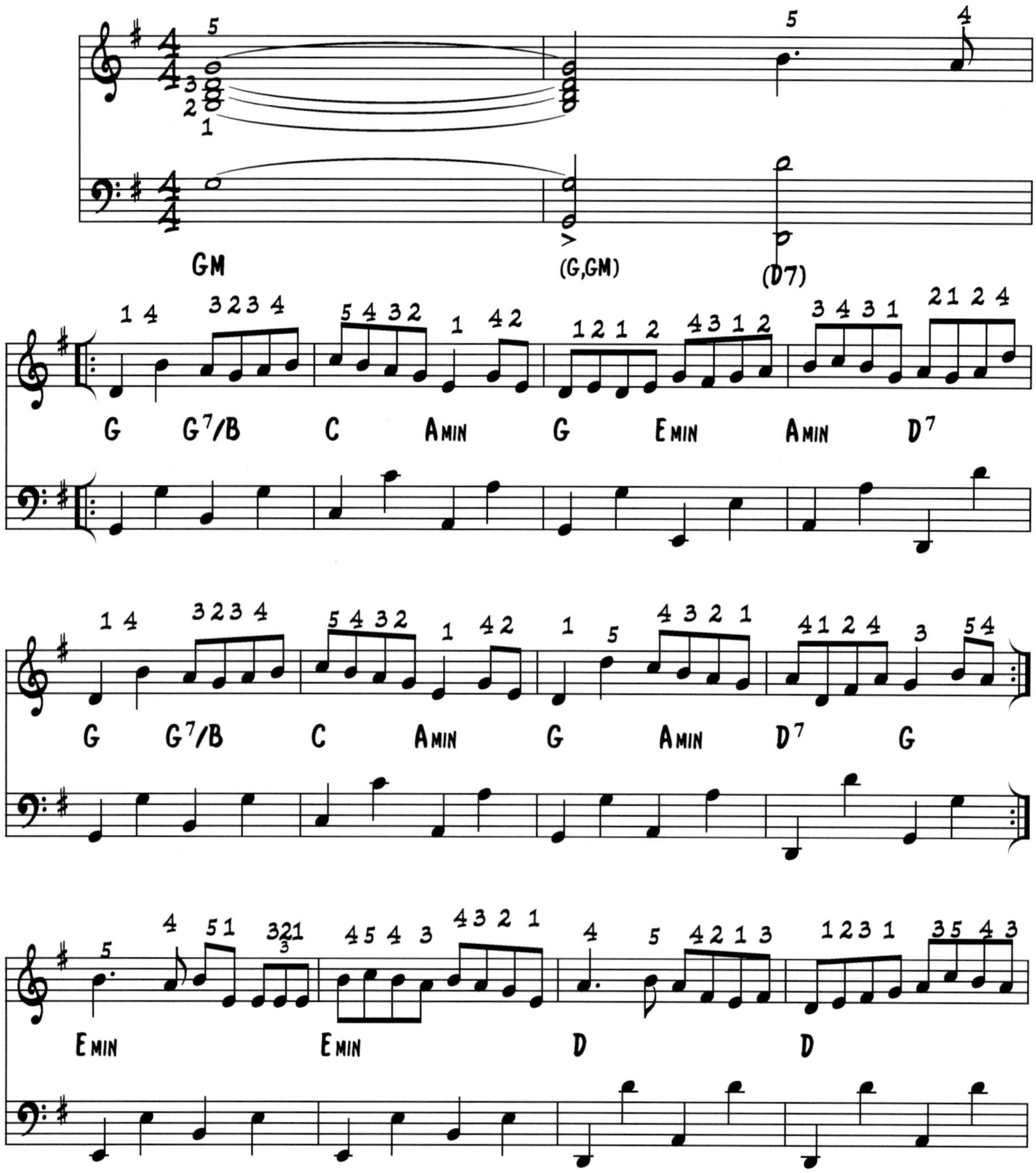

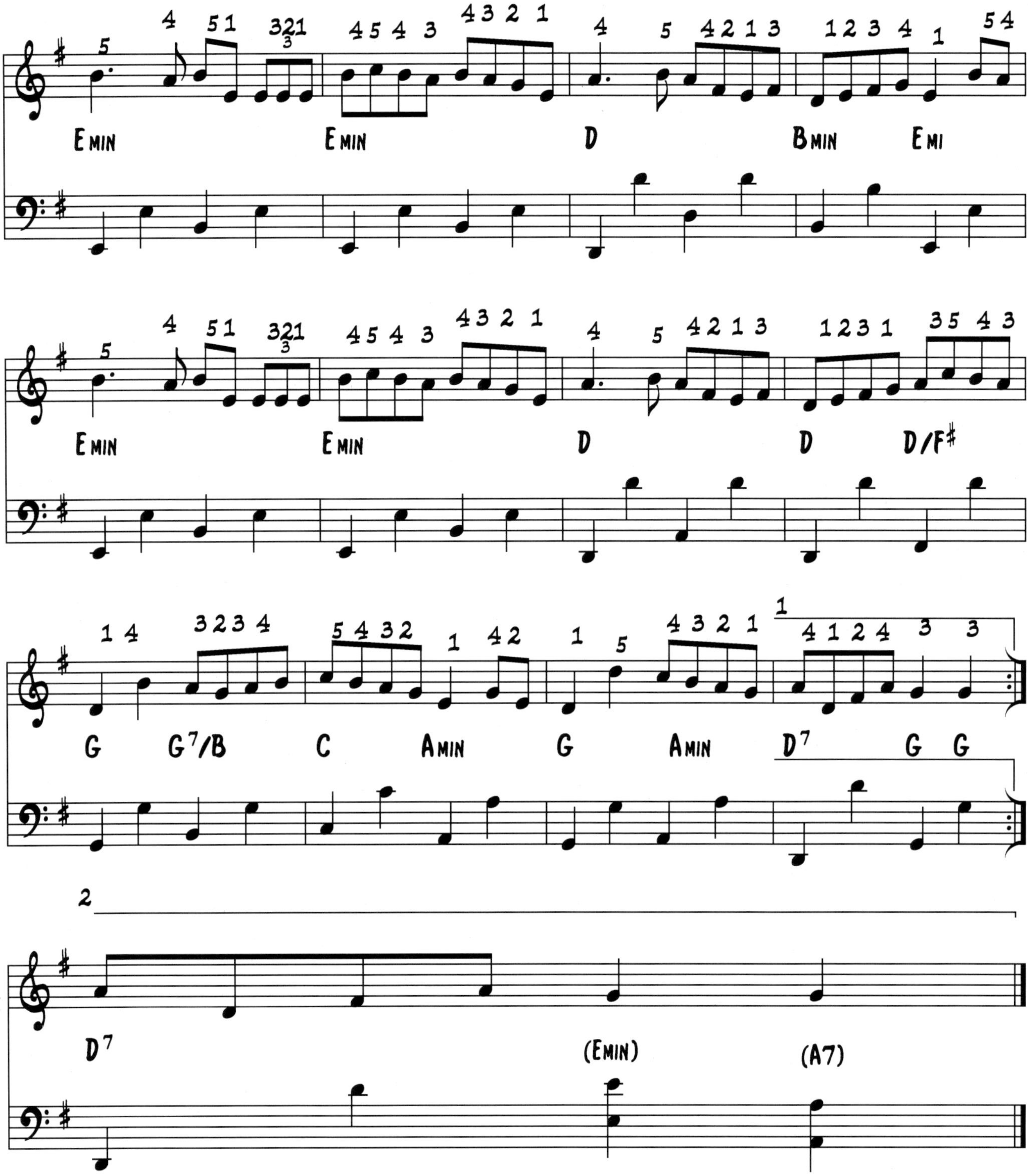
EMIN EMIN D BMIN EMI
EMIN EMIN D D D/F♯
G G7/B C AMIN G AMIN D7 G G
D7 (EMIN) (A7)

The Morning Loop

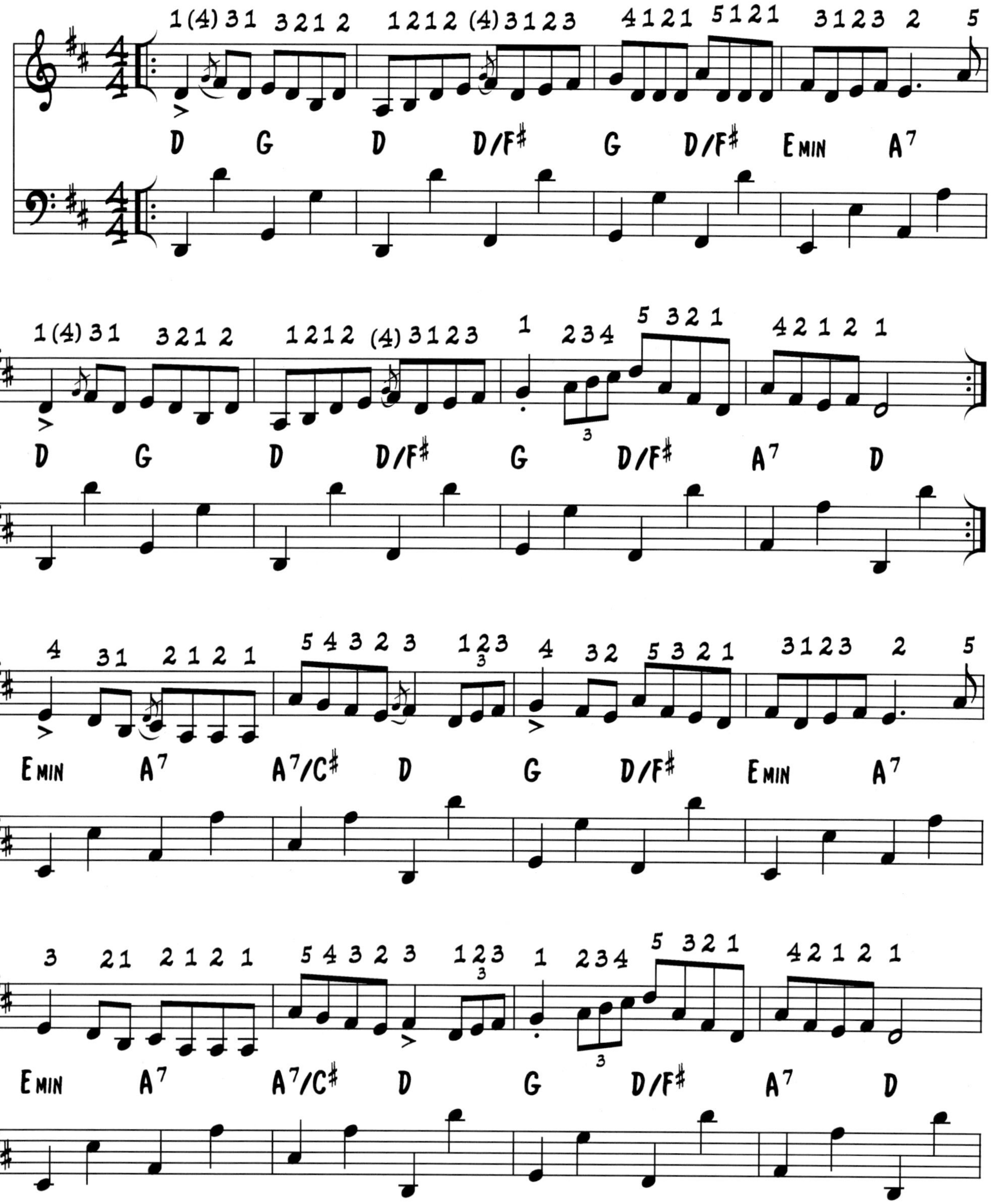

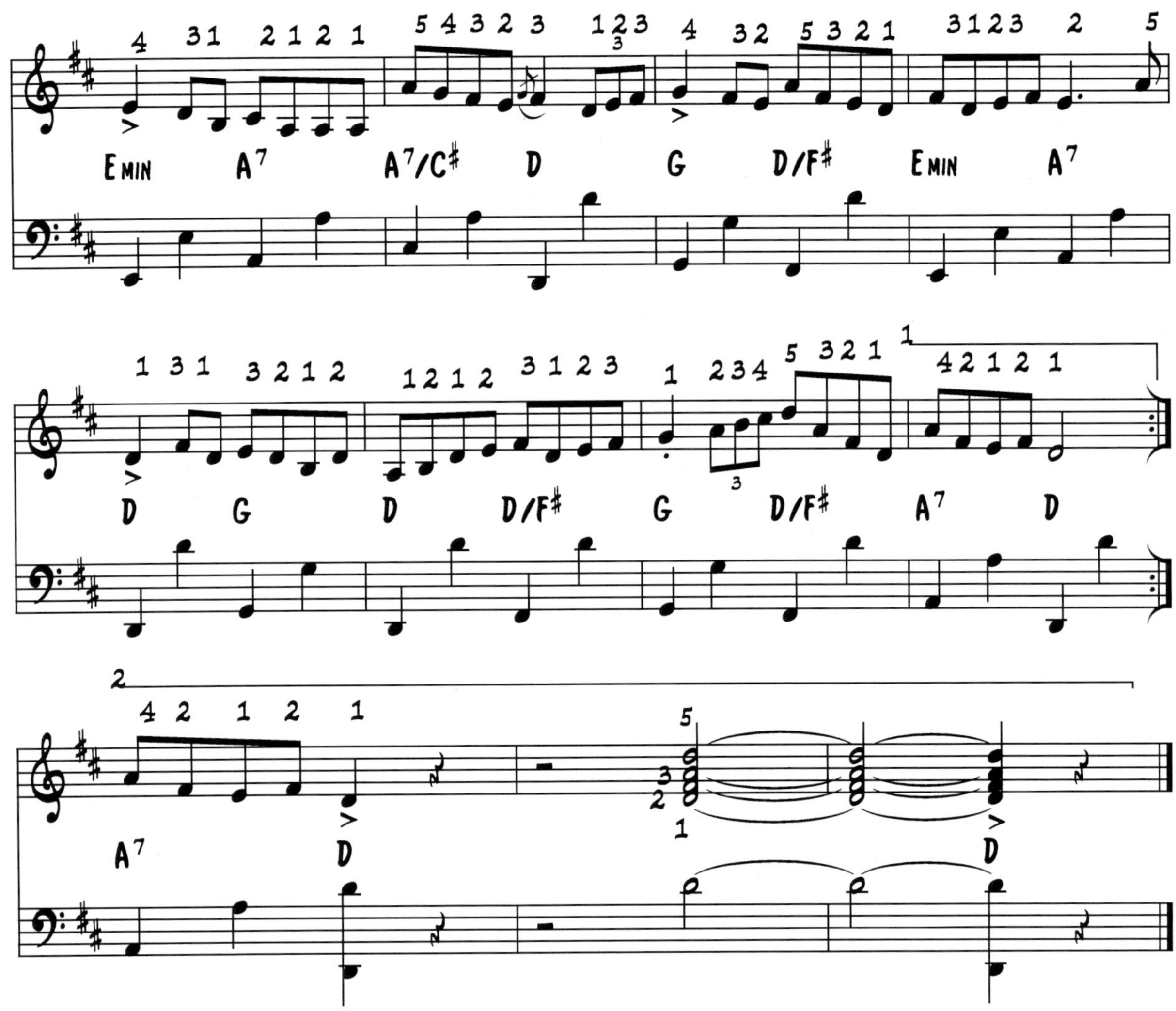

Helpful tips

Now and go explore lots of different tunes and learn them. This book has given you the tools to pick up a traditional Scottish or ceilidh book and learn tunes from it.

Start creating your own sets of tunes and think about how the tunes fit together. Avoid playing tunes in the same key signature but keep tunes in the same style.

If a tune doesn't have chords, work on your harmony and learn about chords. Each note within a scale has a chord. For example. The scale of C major would be C major, D minor, E minor, F major, G major, A minor, B diminished and back to C major. Learn the principal chords for all your scales. These are notated in Roman numerals which name each chord; i, ii, iii, iv, v, vi, vii. viii would be the same as i.

Work hard on your scales and arpeggios as they feature heavily in traditional music. Be comfortable playing any scale with both hands, Major and minor. Recognising scale passages in tunes and using scale fingering will help you to play them.

Listen to other musicians playing in this genre and pick up tunes in the different styles you enjoy. Music is a personal choice and with the resources available to you now, you can listen anywhere.

Lastly, enjoy learning and playing the accordion. It is a fantastic and diverse instrument that can play many different styles of music.

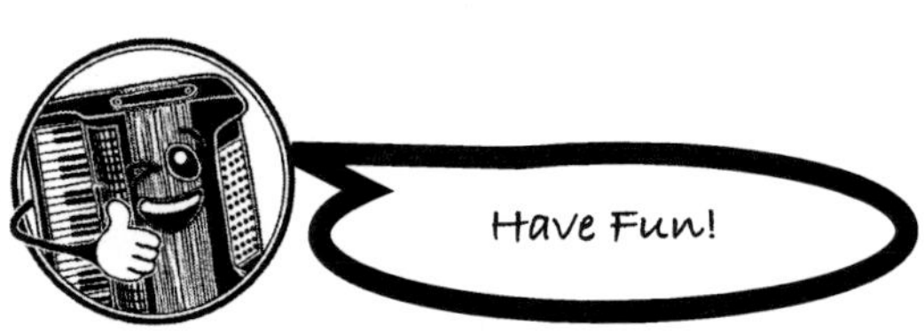

Let's play a Strathspey!

Here is "Lachlan's Bounce" from the strathspey chapter with the performance stylings we have just learned added to it, including the 2-bar introduction motif and a chord at the end.

Ex. 3a is the lead accordion with the band and Ex. 3b is band only.

Ex.3a
Track 61

Ex.3b
Track 62

Lachlan's Bounce

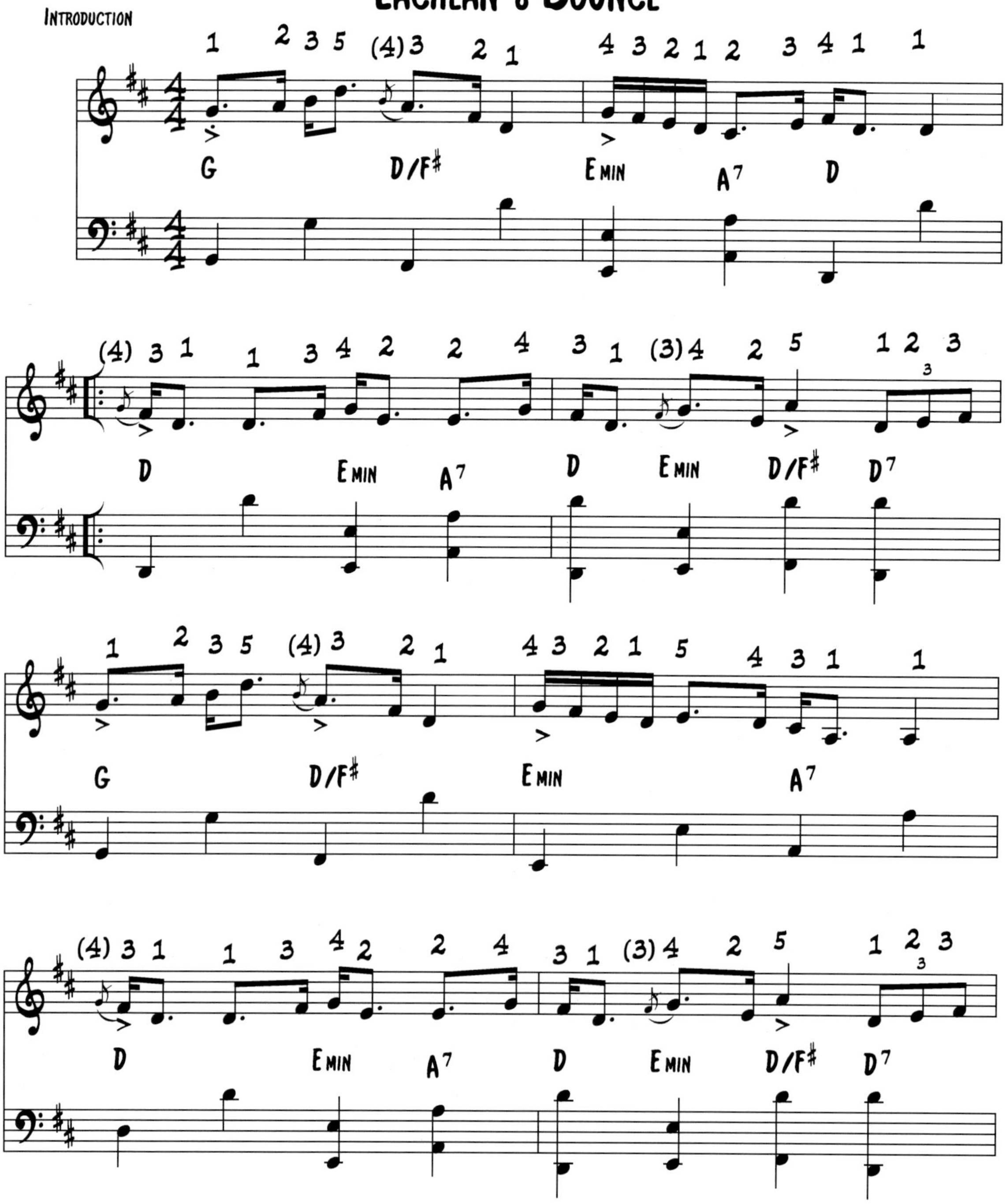

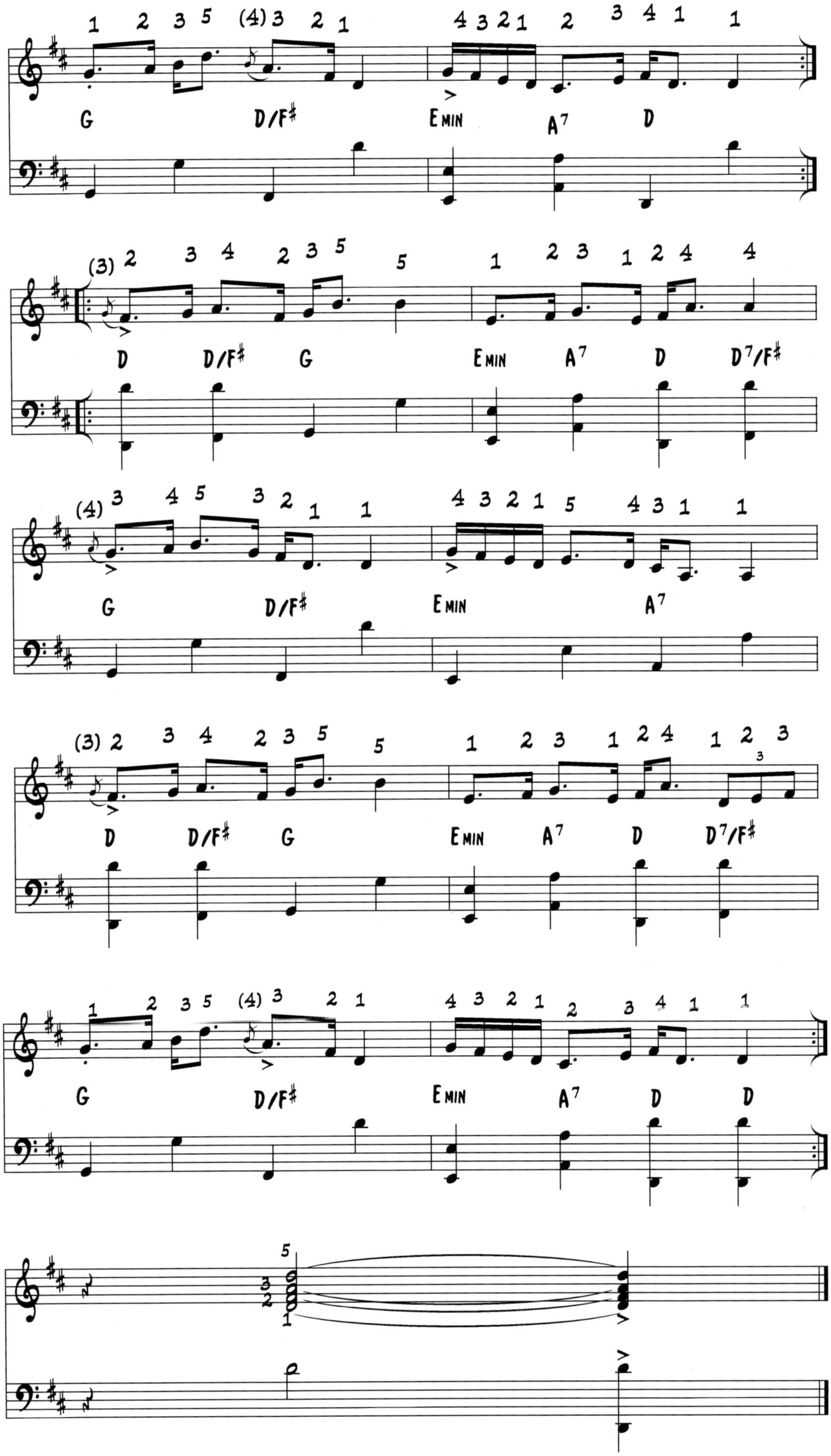
G D/F♯ EMIN A7 D
D D/F♯ G EMIN A7 D D7/F♯
G D/F♯ EMIN A7
D D/F♯ G EMIN A7 D D7/F♯
G D/F♯ EMIN A7 D D

Bass Chart

Counter Bass Row 1

Fundamental Row 2

Major Chords Row 3

Minor Chords Row 4

7th Chords Row 5

Diminished Chords Row 6

Middle C is Here in Row 2

→

Bellows are here on the accordion

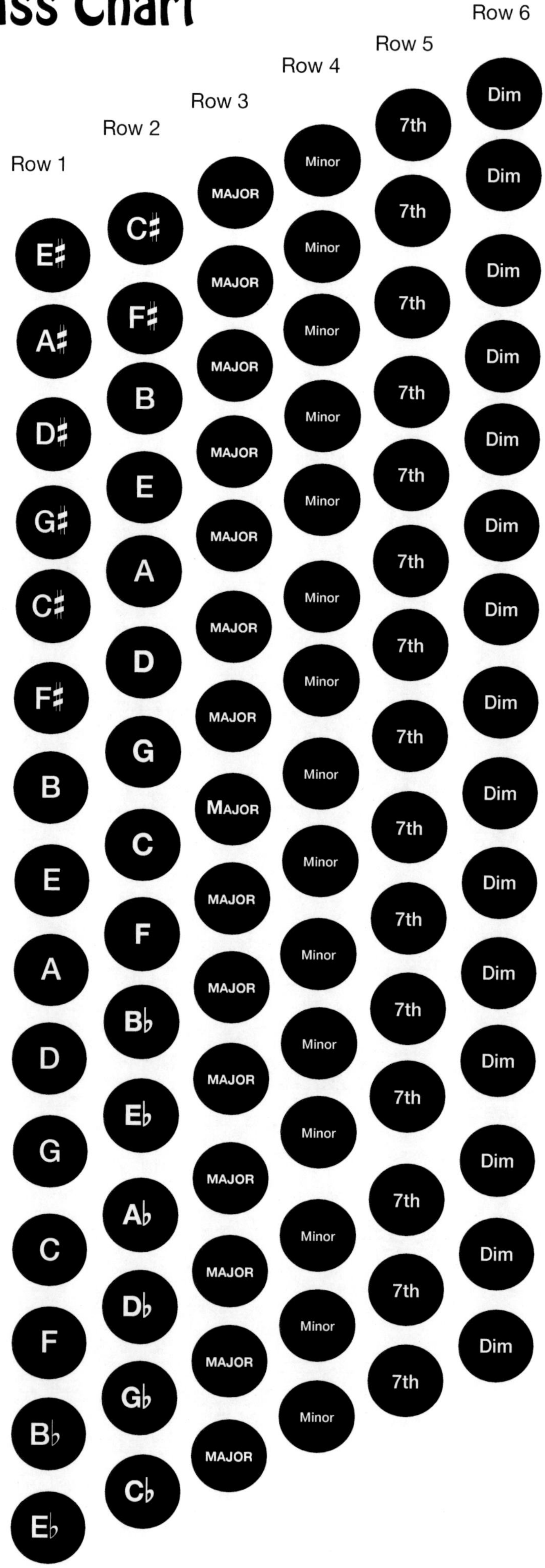

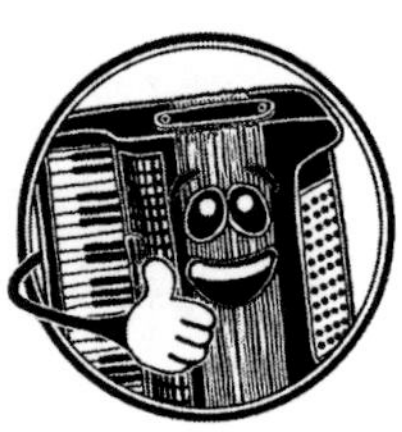

This is not a full-size bass, but there's plenty of information here for traditional music.

About the Author

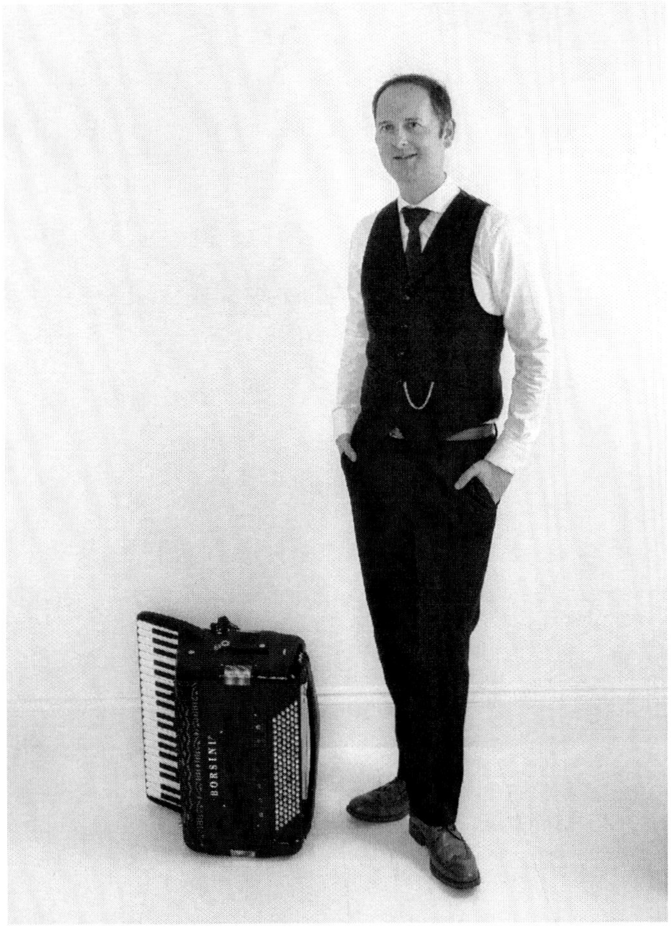

Will Marshall

Based in the Kingdom of Fife in east-central Scotland, Will Marshall is a freelance musical director, composer, musician, and tutor.

With a diverse musical pedigree, Will has several different musical worlds he works in. For many years, he has been the arranger and musical director for the Eden Court Theatre (Inverness) and their pantomime season. Will has also been featured in lots of musical theater shows and is the resident musician for Hebridean Island Cruises.

Traditional music has been a massive part of his life from a young age, ever since studying the accordion with Ian Muir. After success at a major accordion competition, a BBC studio session for "Take the Floor" followed.

Will continued to develop his musical skills and today enjoys working on different studio, theatre, and live session productions. Highlights include BBC Radio 2 "Live with Chris Evans," the arrival of the Olympic flame in the UK with the National Youth Choir of Scotland (ITV), This September, Channel 5. There were also several trips to London for Olympic events: including playing at Scotland House for *Visit Scotland* and The V and A with "The Olympian of the Century," Pele.

As a tutor, Will has created *Learn the Accordion*, a brand-new online platform to help students develop their technique with one-to-one lessons, and a beginners course on its way. He also tutors for Fèis Rois and Angus Council on different projects delivering Scottish music.

As a composer and arranger, Will's work has appeared in ads for *Visit Scotland*, British regional airline, Flybe and TV programs including *The South Bank Show*, and *Ladies of London*, ITV 2.

Other Mel Bay Accordion Books

100 Irish Tunes for Piano Accordion (DiGiuseppe)
100 Tunes for Piano Accordion (DiGiuseppe)
15 Louisiana Cajun Classics for Piano Accordion (Dahl)
A Christmas Tradition: A Celebration with the Accordion (Dahl)
Accordion Music from Around the World (Zucco)
Accordion Uff Da! Let's Dance: Scandanavian Tunes & House Party Music (Bollerud)
Balkan Melodies for Accordion (Irwin)
Cafe Accordion (Newton)
More Cafe Accordion (Newton)
Cajun Spice for Accordion (Hallar)
Clifton Chenier: King of Zydeco (Dahl)
Complete Works of Guido Deiro (Doktorski)
Danse ce soir!: Fiddle and Accordion Music of Quebec (Hart/Sandell)
European Flavor: 14 Accordion Solos on European Melodies (Fazio)
European Flavor II: Accordion Solos (Fazio)
Favorite Accordion Solos (Zucco)
Favorite Hymns and Gospel Songs for Accordion (DiGiuseppe)
French Music for Accordion (Hallar)
French Music for Accordion Volume 2 (Hallar)
French Tangos for Accordion (Dahl)
International Accordion Favorites (Bollerud)
Italian Folk Dances for Accordion (Diianni)
Italian Songs & Arias for Accordion (Dahl)
Jazz Accordion Solos (Dahl)
Russian Melodies for Accordion (Wins)
Solo Accordion Music (Johansen)
Songs of Latin America for Accordion (Troppe)
Songs of Mexico for Accordion (Troppe)
Tangos for Accordion (DiGiuseppe)
Tex-Mex Conjunto Classics for Accordion (Dahl)
The Classical Tradition (Dahl)
Wedding Collection for Accordion (DiGiuseppe)
World Melodies for Accordion (Irwin)